Leadership in the New Century

Gunder Myran
Washtenaw Community College

Tony Zeiss
Central Piedmont Community College

Linda Howdyshell
Washtenaw Community College

Edited by
Bob Greiner
and
Lori J. Sawicki

Published by the
American Association of Community Colleges
National Center for Higher Education
One Dupont Circle, NW, Suite 410
Washington, DC 20036-1176
202/728-0200

Manuscript Editors: Bob Greiner, Lori J. Sawicki, and Ron Stanley
Design: Maryam Makhzani
Cover Design: Gehle Design
Printing: Good Printers

ISBN 0-87117-281-X

CONTENTS
Leadership in the New Century

PREFACE
Leadership in the New Century

We have written this manuscript for community college leaders who are guiding their institutions toward the new century. We too are embarked on this journey, and the insights we share in these pages reflect what we have learned. This book is intended to be more of a handbook than a textbook. We hope that you will find it useful as you work with campus and community groups to design the future of your college, and that it will be of some benefit as you continue your personal leadership journey to the new century.

There is something magical about the year 2000. We hear, as you do, the siren call of new beginnings and new possibilities. We feel we are entering a period of profound and fundamental change for community colleges, the most sweeping period since the 1960s. Then, we transformed from campus-based colleges to community-based colleges; today we are becoming learner-based colleges. As we enter the new century, we will combine the forces of learner-based and community-based education to shape a powerful new definition of the community college.

It seems appropriate that the transition to a new century should also be a period of reframing and reinvention for our society and for community colleges. Those of us who are community college leaders are the stewards of the very precious idea of the open door college—democracy's college—during this pivotal period of the history of our society. What an exciting time to be a community college leader!

We would like to dedicate this manuscript to our mentor and special friend, Professor Max Raines of Michigan State University. The birthplaces of many of the ideas expressed here were Max Raines' classroom and living room. We would also thank the presidents in the COMBASE, League for Innovation, and Continuous Quality Improvement Network organizations for their participation.

CHAPTER 1

Leadership Pathways to the New Century

*"To put it simply, learning is the new form
of labor" (Zuboff, 1988, p. 32).*

INTRODUCTION

This book is about the leadership of fundamental change in the community college. It is about change in the taproots of the organization: its mission and vision, culture, organizational design, and instructional design. It is about governing ideas—those underlying principles, assumptions, and ground rules which determine the daily conduct of the staff and others involved with the college. The book is based on the assertion that community colleges are moving from the community-based paradigm which shaped organizational development for the past thirty years to a new paradigm which combines the forces of learner-based and community-based education to shape a powerful new definition of the new century community college.

The subtitle of this book is "Learning to Improve Learning." The focus is on exploring the learner-based dimension of the new paradigm. It is about the community college leader as learner, staff members as learners, trustees as learners, and organizational learning. It is about student learning, community learning, and staff learning. It is the primary task of community college leaders to ensure continuous improvement of college policies, programs, services, processes, and staff knowledge and skills to increase student learning.

MOVING TO THE LEARNER- AND COMMUNITY-BASED PARADIGM

When the General Motors Corporation was established some eighty years ago, it was the result of bringing together several smaller companies under one roof. This paradigm dominated corporate thinking into the 1980s, even though the market and competitive assumptions on which it was based were no longer valid. For several years after, GM struggled with the transformation to a streamlined, leaner, more competitive organization. And now, as it downsizes and restructures, its paradigm for the new century is emerging.

This pattern—the creation of a formational paradigm, the evolution of external and internal forces that do not fit within it, and the struggle to create a new paradigm—describes the community college. Colleges are moving away from this pattern and struggling to create a new model for the new century.

The old pattern could be called the university/high school outgrowth paradigm. During the first sixty years of existence, community colleges were regarded in many ways as the children of Mother High School and Father University (to borrow from Max Raines). They inherited the production-line rigidity of public schools geared to produce workers for an industrializing nation, and the discipline-based curricular patterns of universities. These influences were instrumental in shaping their social role and the assumptions on which they based curricular, staffing, policy, and financial decisions. This paradigm provided a framework, a set of ground rules, on which to base daily decision making. It gave a sense of predictability regarding the social role and mission of the community college.

The problem with this outgrowth paradigm is the same as for any organizational model. External conditions change, and soon requests for services that do not fit the old pattern emerge: Where do outreach centers in low-income areas fit? Where do customized job training and retraining fit? What about economic development, international education, and technology transfer? In spite of these signals from the external environment, however, the old pattern persists. The community college curriculum still tends to meet such requests with credit-bearing university-transfer courses, or at least courses leading to a degree. In spite of the evidence that most social and economic problems require an interdisciplinary response, the university and the community college tend to cling to the traditional academic-discipline structure. Faculty schedules still tend to fit the high school or university calendar. Some faculty members still think of their external community as their university colleagues rather than the community group that they serve. Universities resist seeing the student as a customer or their enterprise as a business, and this attitude also pervades community colleges.

As the number of uncomfortable questions increases, it becomes more and more apparent that the old set of assumptions and ground rules about the community college mission and what guides its decision making is simply inadequate. The add-ons to the traditional program begin to overwhelm the existing paradigm, and first risk takers and innovators and then the rest of the staff begin to realize that a new model must develop to encompass the emerging external pressure and internal innovations. They begin to realize that if this institutional transformation does not occur, the college will become more and more irrelevant to the educational needs of the community. At some point the college must make a leap of faith from the predictable, comfortable old paradigm to an uncertain yet hopeful new one. The community college model for the new century can be labeled the learner- and community-centered paradigm.

The Old Paradigm: Top-Down Decision Making

Throughout this nation's history, top-down decision making has characterized most of its organizations, including community colleges. As the pace of
social and economic change has accelerated and become less predictable, this
"ivory tower" approach has grown more dysfunctional. The need for organizational flexibility at all levels requires the knowledge, creativity, and problem-
solving skills of all staff members. In addition, college staff expectations of their
involvement in meaningful institutional matters have heightened as leaders across
society move from authoritarian and bureaucratic to collaborative and participative approaches. A community college that has not begun this transformation is
likely to exhibit the following dysfunctions:

- A territorial culture in which all programs compete for limited resources
  and the favor of decision makers
- Reduced communications among staff groups
- Mistrust and low regard for mutual needs
- Too much control by executives
- Too many decisions moving to the top of the organizational structure for
  resolution
- Low staff morale, especially a general feeling of being devalued
- Staff use of avoidance and withdrawal to protest lack of meaningful involve-
  ment

But such a transformation is unlikely to proceed without considerable diffi-
culty. A quick-fix approach, such as forming new staff committees, may create a
short-term appearance of positive change. However, any real solution must
address the fundamental issues of creating a shared mission, reaching consensus
on values and vision, building trust, and developing staff competencies for participative decisions. It must alter organizational culture; the formation of effective
committees is merely one expression of fundamental change.

Innovators cannot assume that such reforms will generate widespread support. There are winners and losers in a top-down culture, and the winners will
resist. Others will simply prefer what is familiar though frustrating to risking
what is promising yet unpredictable. Some may fear that a more participative
environment will require them to expose problem-solving or team-building
weaknesses, or that their own territory will be open to review and discussion by
other staff members.

The New Paradigm: Learner- and Community-Based Leadership

Those involved in community college work in the 1960s will remember its missionary zeal. A new era was beginning as community colleges' doors opened to groups systematically excluded from higher-educational opportunity. The American economy was booming, and these groups were going to get their piece of the economic pie. It was exciting, exhilarating work that had a value-based underpinning. In the 1990s there is a sense of another new but very different era beginning. The problems to be faced are a mix of the new and the old: international competition, the need for revitalization of the public schools, ethnic and racial divisions, polarization between the haves and the have-nots, demands on colleges for public accountability, and calls for leadership in community problem solving. Leadership response to these problems will shape the community college of the new century. As in the 1960s, community colleges are returning to questions of basic purpose.

The new community college leadership model grows out of a new understanding of the place learning fills for people, organizations, and communities. It once was thought that learning had to be experienced on the way to living—a sort of tunnel of schooling to go through in preparation for life. In the recent past, there was talk of lifelong learning—accommodating the role of learner alongside other adult roles such as worker, family member, citizen, and consumer. But now there must be talk of the learning individual, the learning organization, and learning community. Learning must be understood as the heart of all productive activity.

> Learning is no longer a separate activity that occurs either before one enters the workplace or in remote classroom settings. The behaviors that define learning and the behaviors that define being productive are one and the same. Learning is not something that requires time out from being engaged in productive activity; learning is the heart of productive activity. To put it simply, learning is the new form of labor (Zuboff, 1988, p. 32).

The concept that "learning is the new form of labor" for those in roles as worker, family member, citizen, consumer, churchgoer, etc., is a very powerful one for community colleges. Learning is seen not as a preparation for life, or an activity that parallels other adult life roles, but as at the heart of all these. If learning is viewed as a primary endeavor of all adults, underlying and shaping all life roles, how would that change the concept of the community college or, more specifically, community college leadership?

A new model of learner- and community-centered leadership is needed. It is based on the assumption that the best future for community colleges lies in leap-frogging the limitations of excessive bureaucracy, top-heavy administration, and restrictive or self-serving labor-management contracts to a new focus on learning requirements and the success of learners and communities being served. Meeting or exceeding these requirements must drive institutional leadership and development. This new model makes it absolutely clear who the customers of the community college are. It represents a breakthrough from academic tradition that insists, whether admitted or not, that staff preferences take precedence over student or community needs.

Compelling Factors Driving the New Century Leadership Model

No social change drives the new model more than the awareness that economic, social, and technological conditions—from the local to international levels—are certain to change rapidly and unpredictably. The traditional leadership model is too slow in responding to change and does not use the knowledge of all college staff and resources. The future demands short-term strategic alliances among staff groups and between staff and community groups tailored to respond to problems and opportunities as they emerge. The participation of all stakeholders in setting priorities and institutional decision making will be a key feature.

Because community colleges face so many kinds of change within (the diversity of the student body, the specialization of programs and services, and the specialization of staff), it becomes more important to have a unifying sense of institutional purpose, underlying institutional values, and organizational vision for the future. The new model must embrace these centralized and decentralized features.

Another problem is the likelihood, given the long economic restructuring under way in the United States, as well as taxpayer resistance to increased spending for public services, that community college funding will not increase relative to other educational institutions and public services. The new leadership model must include provision for the effective channeling of human, financial, physical, and information resources to maximize their impact on achieving a college's mission.

The assumptions of the old model are familiar and comfortable, although increasingly dysfunctional, but these new assumptions are not nearly so clear. This is the nature of a paradigm shift: the evolutionary point is reached when the old familiar concepts are no longer adequate for the emerging organizational demands, but there is not yet a solid new set to serve as a guidepost for the future. A leap of faith must be made based on a sense of idealism and new imperatives, without clear evidence of the new assumptions' reliability. Like the occupants of a boat crossing a rapidly moving river, who must row as best they can toward the elusive target on the other shore, community college leaders must leave the shore where their boat was safely harbored and head for a still vague and uncertain future.

Comparing Old Leadership Strategies with Strategies for the New Century

The Old Leadership Paradigm	Leadership for the New Century
Focus on plans	Focus on vision
Exclusive involvement in leadership	Inclusive involvement in leadership
Monitoring	Building accountability
Directing	Empowering
Congeniality	Collegiality
Individual performance	Team performance
External leadership	Self-leadership Setting an example Emphasis on moral and ethical conduct Passion and emotion about mission Challenging the process Risk taking Celebration Coaching behavior
Bureaucracy	Team-building, collaboration Community problem solving Emphasis on values
Centralized	Decentralized
Focus on individual learning	Focus on organizational learning Institutional effectiveness and emphasis on continuous quality improvement
Present orientation	Future orientation

The fading community college leadership paradigm assumes that leadership and management are synonymous. Most community college people, when asked to name the college's leadership, would mention the president, other executives, and possibly those playing other organizational roles such as the chairs of the faculty senate or governing board. In the new paradigm, there is a clear difference between management and leadership. While managers have important institutional roles, anyone can be a leader. Leadership will come from faculty members, administrators, office staff, custodial/maintenance staff, students, members of the governing board, and the surrounding community.

COMMUNITY-BASED LEADERSHIP FOR THE NEW CENTURY CAMPUS

Communities have many places of learning: community colleges, universities, private colleges, public schools, businesses, labor unions, governmental units, nonprofit organizations, and many other community groups. There are hundreds of connections among these, which tend to be fragmented. The new century campus will integrate these community learning centers vertically and horizontally.

Vertical Integration

The typical vertical pattern of learning in most communities assumes discrete gaps between K–12, the community college, and the baccalaureate college. A student completes a phase, then faces confusing admissions requirements, frustrating procedures, unexpected prerequisites, and little or no recognition of prior educational work. This creates a disjuncture in the process, and the result may be an unsuccessful transition. Because students may lack this sense of connection, they may drop out of school or have discouraging experiences when reaching the high school-community college disjuncture. This is the old paradigm: learners must work through the maze between educational levels; the individual is responsible, not the system. This procedure is repeated at the community college-baccalaureate college disjuncture. Learners may find that some courses taken at the community college do not transfer to the institutions of their choice.

At the new century campus these gaps are minimized or eliminated. In the community, all levels of education are seen as one community learning system or campus. Those institutions involved in this system will be responsible for creating the connections between levels, whereas this must now be done by the individual student.

An integrated learning system with great potential is the Tech Prep program conceptualized by Dale Parnell, then president of the American Association of

Community Colleges, and sponsored by the federal Perkins Act. The best-known dimension of Tech Prep is the 2 + 2 arrangement that links high school applied-academic courses to technology programs at community colleges. Even more impressive in successful Tech Prep programs is that public schools and community colleges work together to change the way elementary and middle schools prepare students for a future which requires technological awareness and skills in nearly all career areas. Since the 2 + 2 link could eventually be available to fifty percent of secondary school students, Tech Prep may be the new century campus in action.

High school juniors with high grade point averages in academic courses who know which colleges they wish to attend are generally well served by the present system. Such students are unlikely to experience disjuncture between high school and college. High school counselors and college admissions departments ease transitions for academically talented students. But less-directed and less-achieving juniors may not see the connection between their high school work and a community college program, or between their high school experience and a future career. Stronger vertical integration will serve such students well.

Horizontal Integration

Many community organizations are involved in community problem solving. The exact configuration of organizations involved is determined by the nature of the problem. There are many connections between community organizations, but they are not currently thought of as a part of one community learning system. Community problems are approached in a fragmented way with each organization seeking its own ends. The new paradigm will create an integrated system that continuously improves its capacity to solve problems.

International economic competition, the growing gap between haves and have-nots, deep ethnic and racial divisions, and the need for school reform are examples of local and national problems facing community colleges and other social organizations. The problem with the old paradigm of specific programming is the lack of communitywide coordination and cohesiveness. Despite some spectacular successes, most community colleges are still considered to be at the margin of many community problems.

Public school reform is a good example. It is inexcusable that community organizations and groups, including higher education institutions, stand off to the side given the crisis of low student achievement and other deteriorating aspects of America's public schools. Kati Haycock, who heads a school improvement project at the American Association for Higher Education, expresses the role of higher education in this way:

> Many educators, politicians, and much of the public per-
> ceive higher education to be on the sidelines of school
> reform. The problem is that [the array of college programs
> that connect to the schools] are still ad hoc. In any given
> community, you may find hundreds of collaborative ven-
> tures, but they do not add up to a coherent whole (Jacobson,
> 1992, p. A5).

Community colleges have been deeply involved in community problem solving since the social revolution of the 1960s. They play many roles depending on the nature of the problem: leader, catalyst, or educational resource. In the 1960s and 1970s, community-based efforts tended to be limited to programs of continuing education or community service departments, but since then the community-based perspective has permeated nearly all areas of college operations through counseling services, business-industry centers, community relations offices, foundations, regional centers, student volunteer centers, and other operations.

Even so, the struggle continues on many campuses between those who seek a return to more traditional academic programming and those who seek continuing evolution toward community-based programming. Neither of these competing concepts nor some merging of the two is likely to be adequate for the demands of the new century. Society's domestic and international problems are very different from those of the past three decades, and the response must be dramatically different as well. A new paradigm of learner- and community-centered programming is required.

CHAPTER 2

Leadership of Fundamental Change

"For many, reengineering is the only hope for breaking away from the ineffective, antiquated ways of conducting business that will otherwise inevitably destroy them"
(Hammer & Champy, 1993, p. 5).

I t is unfortunate, but community college leaders do not know their business. In response to such a statement most would say, "What? Of course we know our business!" Yet leaders must ask themselves serious questions: Does the community college have a vision statement co-created by the entire college staff? Does the college know who its customers are and their educational requirements? Does it know its products (for example, how well each academic department's offerings match customer requirements)? Does it know whether the benefits produced by each college unit justify the investment made in them? Does it know how well its program development and improvement work, and whether research and development efforts keep pace with changing customer requirements? Does it know whether key processes are aligned to support student-learning improvement? Does it know the degree to which the college's human, financial, physical, and information resources are aligned toward achieving its mission?

Leaders are exposed every day to the language of fundamental change: reengineering, reframing, reinventing, paradigm shift, transformation. Management literature is filled with concepts, principles, and techniques that relate to leading an organization through a period of fundamental change. Because of international competition, the revolution of information technology, the rapidity and constancy of change, and other factors, most business organizations must make fundamental changes in the 1990s to remain competitive and profitable. After taking the position that American companies must throw out old notions about how companies are organized and run and create entirely new ones, Michael Hammer and James Champy (1993, p. 32) put it this way:

> Reengineering, we are convinced, can't be carried out in small and cautious steps. It is an all-or-nothing proposition that produces dramatically impressive results. Most companies have no choice but to muster the courage to do it. For many, reengineering is the only hope for breaking away

from the ineffective, antiquated ways of conducting business that will otherwise inevitably destroy them.

They define reengineering as

the fundamental rethinking and radical redesign of business processes to achieve dramatic improvements in critical, contemporary measures of performance, such as cost, quality, service, and speed.

Fundamental changes in the way business is done are being driven by heightened customer demands, competition, and a changing market. Community colleges are significantly affected by these factors, as are most social institutions. They also are going through a period of fundamental change, and leadership skills and practices are being transformed in response. The authors sent a leadership survey form to every president of the League for Innovation colleges, COM-BASE colleges, and Continuous Quality Improvement Colleagues colleges. Marvin Lane, president of Lamar Community College, Colorado, responded with:

Complexity theory suggests that discovery and re-articulation of the basic rules by which an organization operates actually cause a transformation to take place. This theory indicates that if we want to change the behavior of the organization then we need to change fundamental rules or underlying assumptions of the organization. If instead we dabble in the latest fad, we will capture the attention of a few but most will know that little or no change will take place because the fundamental assumptions or rules haven't changed.

Peter Senge (1990) asks groups of managers to imagine that their organization is an ocean liner. What, he asks, is the leader's role? Captain? Navigator? Helmsman? Senge's answer: designer of the ship. In thinking about the role of leadership in shaping the community college of the new century, the analogy of the ship designer is an accurate one. Just as the designer determines the ship's capacity, power, and maneuverability, the community college leader must provide leadership for the fundamental design of the community college of the future. The design's elements can be categorized as follows:

A. Personal mastery
    • Personal mastery of the leaders
    • Personal mastery of all staff members

B. Governing ideas
    • Mission and values
    • Shared vision
    • Indicators of effectiveness
    • Outcomes of significance

C. Key processes
    • Academic development
    • Master class schedule
    • Strategic and annual planning and budgeting
    • Student progress flow through programs and services
    • Student registration
    • Policy development
    • Instructional support
    • Staff recruitment, orientation, professional development, and evaluation
    • Community development and leadership

D. Cultural change
    • Building departmental and unit teams
    • Building cross-functional teams
    • Building community within the college
    • Building community networks

Personal Mastery

College leaders, like most professionals, tend to separate their personal lives from their professional lives. Their personal worlds never interfere with leadership responsibilities. However, personal values and experiences have a direct impact on leadership style, behavior, and effectiveness. "Private victories," to use Stephen R. Covey's term, must precede "public victories." Covey (et al., 1994, p. 281) studied two hundred years of leadership research and determined that highly effective people have a foundation of personal strengths that permit them to move effectively from dependence to independence to interdependence. They achieved a balance among personal needs, love and support of family, personal relationships, and public life. Of the "seven habits of highly effective people" that he identifies, four relate to personal attributes: proactivity based on self-chosen values; a personal vision that provides meaning, purpose, and direction to one's life; saying "yes" to that which is truly important (or "putting first things first"); and continuous improvement in physical, mental, spiritual, and social/emotional dimensions.

Presidents who responded to the authors' survey engage in a wide range of self-renewal activities. James Linksz of Bucks County Community College, Pennsylvania, volunteers as an emergency medical technician and EMT trainer, and participates in Habitat for Humanity home construction projects. David Ponitz of Sinclair Community College, Ohio, spent time in India as part of a World Bank project. Stephen Pannill, interim president of Hartford Community College, Maryland, takes extended backpacking trips. Nearly all respondents said they are reenergized through reading and attending leadership seminars. And yet, "putting first things first" is a struggle for most community college leaders. Walter Bumphus of Brookhaven College, Texas, states:

> I have to purposefully schedule times for myself which allow me to reflect, meditate, exercise, and grow intellectually. Because schedules are so intense, balance is critical. Keeping work-related components in check and making time for oneself can lead to fresh perspectives, renewed interest, energy to continue, and thoughtful, sound decision making.

The remaining three habits, while in the dimension Covey calls "public victory," also relate to personal mastery: seeking mutual benefit in all relationships; reflecting first an understanding of others when responding; and valuing others' opinions, viewpoints, and perspectives when seeking solutions.

Most college leaders would probably agree that there is a strong relationship between their private and public victories. It is interesting, then, how rarely in community college leadership literature this connection is recognized. Many college administrators take pride in extraordinarily long work hours and not taking vacation time. It is simply impossible to give unendingly. Everyone needs time for replenishment of spirit and body. Everyone needs time for refreshment, reflection, and renewal. This is especially true for those who would lead fundamental change. Continuous self-renewal is a prerequisite to the leadership of institutional renewal.

In addition to achieving personal mastery, community college leaders of the new century must create organizational environments that support the personal mastery of staff members. As leaders learn to emphasize individuals more than the positions they hold, colleges will benefit from talents and insights that grow out of many kinds of experiences. The self-renewal of staff members is a prerequisite to organizational renewal.

Senge (1994a) adds another element to personal mastery with his emphasis on personal vision as a stepping stone to developing an organizational vision statement. In a recent videoconference he described an organization in which every staff member developed a personal vision statement as part of such a process. These statements captured what each individual envisioned as a preferred future of the organization. They were then displayed and all staff were involved in deriving from them a collective vision. While a number of community colleges have organizational vision statements, it is probably quite rare to have these statements grow out of individual statements. Yet the sense of personal mastery that can result from having one's own vision contribute to the organizational vision will benefit each individual and the college.

Governing Ideas

The very notion of the "governing ideas" of a community college may strike some as a bit strange. Leaders may take governing ideas for granted, or may be so burdened with operational matters that little thought is given to what fundamental ideas underlie daily activities. When leading fundamental change, however, these governing ideas become essential building blocks. They will determine the shape and substance of all future design elements.

Mission and values. A mission statement is the most enduring and unchanging statement of a college's social purpose. To be an instrument of fundamental change, it must be both memorable and "remembrable." Everyone must internalize the statement and use it as a guide for actions and decision making if it is to influence change.

Creating a shared vision. The conditions for fundamental change in a community college rarely occur. A crisis such as a major labor-management conflict or a massive local economic turndown can force it. Most of the time, however, the desire for equilibrium limits the readiness for fundamental change. In looking toward the new century, another possible impetus for change is seen: a compelling vision that all involved have created together to which they devote their talent and energy.

Indicators of effectiveness. An important innovation in community colleges that connects to the vision statement is indicators of effectiveness and related measurements. Spawned by requirements of accreditation and governmental agencies, these indicators provide verifiable criteria to judge the progress of a college in achieving its goals. In an era when the public, employers, and government demand greater accountability, these indicators and the related measures provide standards for accomplishment.

Indicators of effectiveness might include statistics on whether graduates of the college get the jobs for which they have been prepared, and employers are satisfied with the graduates' performance.

Related measurements would include graduate follow-up studies, employer satisfaction studies, and job market surveys.

Outcomes of significance. To carry out a college's vision, a small number of key outcomes must be accomplished during a given period of the college's development. If the vision is to be achieved during the next five years, what are the key conditions that must exist at the end of that time? For example, at Washtenaw Community College, Michigan, two of the outcomes for 2000 are:

- We continuously learn how to improve our performance at each stage of the student's flow through college programs and services.
- We work in teams and help one another to be successful.

These and six more represent decisions about significant changes that will occur at the college within the next five years. Strategic goals specify more concretely how each outcome will be created.

Five to ten outcomes should be planned. If more seem necessary, those involved have not yet organized their goals around the truly critical desired outcomes. Remember, the focus is fundamental change. That is why the term "outcomes of significance" rather than "strategic goals" has been chosen.

Key processes. There are probably nine or ten key processes that drive the achievement of any college's vision. The list provided earlier in this chapter probably would apply, with some variation, to most community colleges. These cross-functional processes depend on the cooperation of several units of the college. Their continuous improvement requires rethinking how work gets done. This shift involves moving from a mental model based on the dominance of a vertical structure (position descriptions, reporting relations, and organization charts) to the dominance of a horizontal structure. A horizontal model cuts across the vertical and breaks down the walls between its units or "silos." By cooperating with other units, staff members learn to see their own responsibilities as part of a larger system, and that helping others to succeed aids their own causes. Involvement in cross-functional teams that work to continuously improve key processes aligns the work of the college to achieving student success and other dimensions of a college's mission.

Cultural change. New century innovators must deal with the attitudes and assumptions staff members have about "how things really work around here." Do people have to guard what they say, or can they express their opinions without fear of repercussion? Are the executives trustworthy? Can one risk failure? Is hard work really expected, and does it lead to a difference in treatment? Is one's work really respected and will he or she be recognized for going the extra mile? The comments that staff members exchange about such questions in the hallways and dining rooms determine the culture more than pronouncements from presidents or other executives.

Managing cultural change is extremely difficult because it deals with what staff members carry in their minds and hearts. It takes place one person at a time. If the staff views the college culture as fraught with danger and frustration, a leader must demonstrate through action that those who take risks are not punished, and that those who work hard are not ignored. Over time, staff members will change their underlying assumption, based on dependable evidence that it is no longer valid, thereby changing the culture of the organization.

CHAPTER 3

Social Forces Driving Fundamental Change

"Two converging forces—a skilled worker shortage, and the development of a perma- nent under class—are bearing down upon the United States" (Dale Parnell, 1990, p. 103).

I n many respects, America's social challenges have never been greater. Soci- ety faces increasing crime, national debt, and demands on government—all of which threaten the economy. The breakdown of the family unit is cause for tre- mendous social concern. Community colleges' task of producing well-educated, productive citizens seems almost impossible. The problems facing business are equally foreboding. One common foe of government, dysfunctional families, education, and business is illiteracy—in basic, technical, and communication skills. To combat this enemy, there must be fundamental change in the methods of higher education. Fortunately, the tools to perform the task are available, but transforming any educational organization is difficult even in the best of circum- stances. Nonetheless, America's community colleges must rise to the occasion, shed anything that limits effective service of students and communities, and transform their thinking and their delivery of education.

Society must educate well to live well. The ability to equip all people with the knowledge and skills to be productive is what community colleges and higher education must be about. If the United States hopes to remain the leading demo- cratic society and the most prosperous, it must have a workforce and supportive business climate that allow it to outperform other countries. It must give hope to all residents for their share of prosperity. Community colleges offer such hope and will play an increasingly critical role in the nation's well-being if they seize this opportunity to meet these emerging needs.

In this last decade of the twentieth century, human development—the most important business of today's society—will rise to the top of the national agenda. Dale Parnell (1990, pp. 240, 250) outlines this problem by explaining that "two converging forces—a skilled worker shortage, and the development of a perma- nent under class—are bearing down upon the United States." He explains that a major challenge for the 1990s will be to solve this problem by completely engaging colleges and universities. If society plans to expand or even maintain its prosperity, it must address the fundamental ways higher education serves business, government, and students. To ignore this would guarantee a reduced standard of living and the development of a large underclass population, little or no middle class, and an elite upper class.

THE NEW ECONOMY—A CALL FOR ACTION

The United States faces some unprecedented challenges to its economy. International competition, an expanded common market, and increasing domestic problems force new demands on the fundamental structures of government and higher education. Government is grappling with runaway debt, flat revenues, and enormous demands for increased services. Health care costs and infrastructure deterioration are escalating the need to reevaluate government services and the way the government budgets its resources. Community colleges are not immune to the effects of these national problems, nor to decreasing revenues and increasing community expectations. They, especially, are expected to provide expanded services to immigrants, dislocated workers, single parents, and the homeless, while continuing the basic mission of providing quality technical/professional and academic transfer programs.

Thomas Gonzalez (1991) vividly documents concerns about the nation's ability to compete and concludes that if productivity continues to falter, the United States could expect one of two futures: either the richest thirty percent of the population would grow wealthier and the rest progressively poorer, or everyone would slide into relative poverty together. One solution is a high-skill, high-work model, which can only be developed through a better-educated and better-trained population. Gonzales—a member of the commission appointed by the National Center for Education and the Economy, which published the *America's Choice* report—says no educational institutions are better suited to assisting the broad-based national implementation of the commission's recommendations than community colleges because they are located within commuting distance of more than ninety percent of America's population.

The integration of higher education and business is essential. Anthony Carnevale (1991) accurately describes the challenges as the country shifts to a globalization of wealth and competition. In this new economy, he says, organizations and nations must be concerned not only with productivity, but with quality, variety, customization, convenience, and timeliness. The demands of this new economy require workers skilled at learning and analytical thinking.

Although people commonly solicit their government for personal wealth and jobs, history has proven that such economic models do not work. The nation's power and wealth simply are not driven by government. They are driven by individuals and their collective ability to compete in the world marketplace. All Americans must gain the knowledge, skills, and motivation to be the world's best workers and most creative thinkers. As the United States progresses through the nineties, human development will rise to the top of the national agenda, and President Clinton's economic proposals recognize this need. Success will depend on two fundamental issues: Whether America's higher education institutions will accept a greater role in providing educational services to meet business needs, and whether government at all levels will allow higher education the autonomy and flexibility to meet them. As resources tighten, flexible partnerships between business and education will become more desirable, yet many government leaders, especially at the state level, will inevitably continue proposing greater centralization of higher education governance and curriculum control. This is producing an ideological collision course.

Society needs only to look at the paralysis in government to envision what its colleges will be like if current "controlling" trends continue. The United States has 125 federal training programs administered by fourteen federal departments or agencies. The funding for these programs exceeds $16 billion (Maynard, 1993). Unfortunately, these programs are beset with duplication, patronage, and unbelievable bureaucracy. President Clinton, like George Bush before him, recognizes the problems of federal job training programs and has proposed ways to clean up the system. Three years have lapsed, however, without any new legislation.

Predictably, confusion and bureaucracy eventually limit the success of any system that evolves in a fragmented manner and is driven by political interests rather than marketplace needs. This creates a dilemma for elected officials, who are besieged with requests to fix today's most pressing problems. They respond with generally well-legislated programs designed to provide immediate short-term solutions. Unfortunately, good initial legislation often generates bad long-term policy. Well-intended and successful federal programs continue operating long after their need or effectiveness has passed, and programs are created on top of these to correct deficiencies.

America's business sector continues to recognize the training and educational needs of its employees. *Training Magazine* consistently reports that American businesses spend $40–60 billion annually to train their employees. These business leaders understand that people drive their profits and that the only way their companies can remain competitive is with fair prices and quality. Some recognizable trends include management providing more training for on-line workers; workers managing themselves with less supervision; public higher education institutions providing more work-site education and training; and public-private partnerships becoming the norm for development efforts.

A recent cover story in *Nation's Business* reported that by 2000, according to the American Society for Training and Development, more than sixty-five percent of all jobs will require some education beyond high school, twenty-three million people will be employed in the technical area, and nearly fifty million workers will need upgraded skills training to perform their current jobs (Szabo, 1993).

These trends indicate that business, government, and education recognize that the world is entering a new economic age. This economy will require adjustment in the way education is delivered. New models for integrating education, technology, and business are being developed and are successful. Educators are beginning to understand that they cannot exist in a vacuum, must be accountable for their product, and live in a global village. Business leaders are beginning to understand that the collective skills of their workers and a flexible team approach for achieving continuous quality improvement are essential to their survival. Government leaders seem to acknowledge that education and training are two of the most important American businesses. As the country adjusts to this new economy and its internationally competitive nature, its community colleges should and must be at the forefront.

This new age represents a serious call for community colleges to expand their missions to include permanent, direct association with economic development. Human development is their primary business. In this respect, there is no difference between economic and human development, since it is people's ability to produce that drives the economy. William Kolberg and Foster Smith (1992) reveal that America is failing to stay abreast of the times, its students are not as educated as many foreign students, its workers are underskilled, and its businesses have not been as efficient as many foreign competitors'. They surmise that uncorrected, these problems will undermine America's economic foundation. Kolberg and Smith also note that America's businesses are changing through investment in people and reorganizing in a decentralized, entrepreneurial fashion to become more efficient.

The National Education Goals Panel recently produced its first report on the progress toward six goals set by the National Governors' Association for achievement by 2000. The fifth goal is to make all American adults literate and ensure that they have the knowledge and skills to compete in a global economy.

The mandate is obvious. Business and government want a change in the way America educates. It appears that those who are responsible for education should listen and change, or someone—most likely the government—will make the changes without them.

Financial, political, and social benefits abound for colleges that shift or expand their efforts toward making this nation's economy the strongest in the world. This is not to suggest that teaching arts and humanities should suffer at the expense of technologies and new basic skills. Rather, as two-year colleges join with business to work more closely with government-driven training programs, they will find more resources to support the total curricula of their schools.

Fortunately, community colleges long ago discovered the wide-ranging benefits of becoming client-centered, market-driven, and highly integrated with business. The general respect and support for colleges from the private and the public sectors have increased in direct proportion to their emergence as America's most successful workforce-development institutions. Still, change and practical political positioning must occur at the community college if these institutions hope to meet the nation's current challenges and reap the associated benefits.

As the United States continues to shift its foreign and domestic attention toward international competition, education and business integration will grow in importance. Eventually, America will export its education and training expertise to "most favored nations" to help ensure their economic vitality. Americans are faced with clear challenges: if they want to live well, they must produce well; if they want to produce well, they must educate well. All sectors of society seem to acknowledge the need for a seamless relationship between education and business, fully supported by all levels of government. Scores of national reports on the subject have been published in recent years, and the White House and the National Governors' Association developed and are promoting a set of clear, practical, and measurable educational goals. The motivation behind this flurry of national activity is the recognition that people and their abilities to produce are what ultimately drive the economy—not corporate structures, and not government.

Education must not exist in a vacuum. It has a compelling obligation to change with the needs of business and the society it serves. In this time of monumental upheaval in governments and their economic systems, it is safe to assume that change will become the norm. New needs lead to rising expectations and call for different strategies to meet them. America's community colleges should be at the forefront in designing and delivering those strategies.

CHAPTER 4

Shaping the Culture

"It must be considered that there is nothing more difficult to carry out, nor more doubtful of success, nor more dangerous to handle than to initiate a new order of things"
—Niccolo Machiavelli (Kayser, 1990, p. ix).

The concept of culture, although popular as a way of explaining organizational phenomena, has been difficult to define, analyze, and measure, and even harder to manage. Community college leaders find that the study of their organization's culture, despite its complexity, will illuminate breakdowns between subgroups that are more than communication problems or a lack of teamwork. Edgar H. Schein (1992, p. 48) writes, "We must come to understand fully what culture is in human groups, organizations, and nations so that we can have a deeper understanding of what goes on, why it goes on, and what, if anything, we can do about it."

Most community colleges established twenty to thirty years ago have cultures. Whether they are desirable ones—providing satisfactory climates for learning and responding—is debatable. Some have developed cultures which reinforce the status quo, restrict creativity, and stifle innovation. In many places, institutional cultures are characterized as formal, stifling, and joyless—exactly the opposite of the work environment most people want.

Organizational learning, continuous quality improvement (CQI) initiatives, and other planned changes cannot be understood without considering culture as a primary stabilizing force. The level of resistance from within an organization to becoming more effective—even in times of threatened survival—amazes many leaders. Schein states that the ability to step outside the culture, perceive its limitations, and develop a new culture is the ultimate challenge of leadership.

DEFINING CULTURE

The term "organizational culture" generally refers to the shared beliefs and understandings held by a particular group about its problems, practices, and goals (Reicher and Schneider, 1990). For example, in unionized settings faculty members and administrators are oriented to believe in a "we versus they" framework. Both groups feel devalued and retreat into safe behaviors. Both understand the unwritten rules. Culture results from a group learning process. For group learning to occur, there must be a history of shared experience which implies some stability of membership. As groups grow, subcultures develop with their own shared histories and norms. Strong divisional subcultures are not a problem unless implementation of common practices is a goal, through continuous quality improvement or a strategic plan.

Some cultures define themselves in terms of their opposition to other groups. For example, some unions form in opposition to management and assume that management and labor are structurally and permanently in conflict. Elements of culture are observable standards of dress, language, and behavior; the way group members interact; their special competencies, mental models, habits, and values; and symbols. All of these elements contribute to the culture, but are not the culture.

Schein contends that the concept of organizational culture often is misunderstood and is confused with the related concepts of climate, ideology, and style. Culture is sometimes defined in terms of overt organizational behavior; organizational ideology and philosophy; group and organizational norms; espoused organizational values; policies, procedures, and rules of socialization; and climate.

These terms define components of culture, but don't really focus on the essence of real organizational culture. According to Schein, culture adds two elements: structural stability and a pattern or integration that ties together all other components. Organizational culture provides stability to organizations. It establishes a pattern of interactions. In many community colleges, despite organizational restructuring, the division between faculty and administration continues. Each day hundreds of people repeat past behaviors by communicating and behaving in familiar ways. Staff sometimes unite against other departments with conflicting interests. Culture, Schein says, is the accumulated shared learning of a given group, covering behavioral, emotional, and cognitive elements of its members' total psychological functioning.

Culture, then, is the interaction of internal integration and external adaptation. The college learns to accomplish tasks that enable it to serve the changing needs of its students while developing and maintaining internal relationships. The processes that build and develop the group occur alongside problem solving and task accomplishment. It is easy to understand why groups rely on the past for information and predictability. No one wants to reinvent the wheel, as there is little enough time or energy for faculty to adapt to the ever-changing external environment.

Internal integration creates a common language, defines group boundaries and criteria for inclusion and exclusion, distributes power and status, develops norms for friendship, and allocates rewards and punishments. The assumptions that leaders take for granted are passed on through daily decisions. Thus organizational culture becomes a "normative glue" (Morgan, 1986) that structures the milieu and makes it possible for people to derive meaning from their labors, work comfortably with others, and focus on key organizational tasks.

HOW CULTURES ORIGINATE

The learning process for groups starts with a boom. Faculty and staff propose programs and courses of action and are extremely successful. As group problems are solved, a set of shared assumptions forms. Solutions tend to be taken for granted and defended rather than examined as the culture coalesces. These assumptions work well enough that they are taught to new members. The culture provides stability, predictability, and meaning as a result of effective functional decisions or actions in the group's past. Like a coin, culture has two sides. The negative side means that leaders discount innovation with "That's not how we do things." Peer pressure falls unrelentingly on those who break out of the mold. Institutional methods are so ingrained that few even think of doing things another way. As a result, group learning slows, as does improvement.

THE FUNCTION OF CULTURE

Asking voters to approve additional operating millage because of an increasing student body once was an effective functional decision. In areas where community colleges are partly funded through property taxes, that decision resulted in increased millage. In recent years an antitax sentiment has increased. *The Chronicle of Higher Education* (1995) editorially states that "the compact" under which each generation pays to educate the subsequent generation has been abandoned. Business and government employees are applying total quality management techniques to increase efficiency and improve effectiveness. The past assumption that voters would want to pay to educate less fortunate members of their community or provide a higher level of service may be less valid today.

Another assumption is that students will continue to come to community colleges because they are inexpensive. This niche has produced more than enough students in the past. However, government and accrediting agencies are starting to require proof of learning. Consumers as a whole will not continue to buy ineffective services no matter what the price.

As leaders recognize that the external environment and customers' demands are changing, a struggle results. Stability is sought within the college and it becomes easier to distort new data by denial rather than by changing basic assumptions. It will be difficult for leaders to learn new ways, and even more difficult for group members who have grown complacent.

ORGANIZATIONAL LIFE CYCLE

To understand cultural change, it is necessary to examine what happens when any group develops. According to Ichak Adizes (1988), the growth and aging of an organization are primarily manifested in the interrelationship between flexibility and controllability. He lists three stages: the founding and developing age when organizations are very flexible, but not very controllable; midlife, when the organization is both flexible and controllable; then maturity and decline, when the organization becomes inflexible and very controlling. Age is not the sole determinant of effectiveness, but rather of an organization's ability to plan changes. The notion that new leaders become cultural-change agents declines as organizations mature.

CULTURAL LEADERSHIP

Building an effective organization requires the rallying of diverse subgroups around common goals, language, and processes. An organization learns only when its leadership learns. Leaders must have new insights to explore new learning. Morgan says successful leadership depends on an ability to create or maintain shared reality and meaning. Culture can restrict an organization's ability to assess changes and adapt appropriately. K.E. Weick (1990) asserts that it is difficult to separate strategic change from cultural change.

Schein (1992) believes a shared understanding of core mission and primary tasks is the key to developing consensus on the appropriate repair goals. The mission is the most fundamental expression of the college's purpose. It balances student learning needs, faculty development, financial security, and community demands to develop a highly skilled labor force. Successful leaders keep all stakeholders' needs in balance.

A learning leader must perceive environmental changes and their implications for the organization, and provide enough discomforting information to unfreeze complacency. The anxiety created must be acknowledged, and a vision of the future and how to reach it must be provided. The telling and selling of the vision are required of leaders who want to change the culture.

Reactions to change can be comparable to psychologist Elizabeth Kubler-Ross' stages of dying. These phases are denial, resistance, exploration, and commitment. Even positive changes bring a "letting go" of the familiar and require time.

Communication and information are central to a learning culture. Everyone must be able to communicate with everyone else to assume that telling the truth is desirable. Information is critical to effective problem solving and learning.

Leaders often find that any attempt to change an organization's basic functions must be counter-culture. Organizational change programs are usually brief because they manipulate some cultural elements while leaving others constant. For example, presidents may see the value of using teams to solve problems at the implementation level, but sometimes these teams communicate only between organizational chart boxes, in the connecting white spaces. If the reward system, the reporting relationship, and the accountability system are based on individualistic assumptions, teamwork will be subverted.

To manage culture, a leader must reconstruct the history of how the group solved its major problems of external adaptation and internal integration. That leader must also focus on which kinds of solutions worked repeatedly and became embedded. This information needs to be raised to the surface and discussed in light of the changing environment and different customer needs.

Kotter (1992) found that strong cultures which were able to adapt to changing environments had a set of interlocked core beliefs about the importance of people, meeting the needs of all stakeholders, and perpetual learning and change. Community college leaders must foster such strong cultures to fulfill their missions.

CHAPTER 5

The Power of Vision

"A shared vision is not an idea. It is not even an important idea such as freedom. It is, rather, a force in people's hearts, a force of impressive power. At its simplest level, a shared vision is the answer to the question, 'What do we want to create'" (Peter Senge, 1990, p. 206)?

Developing and implementing a shared vision is one of the key instruments for fundamental change in community colleges. Through the power of a compelling vision, the staff and others involved can move from seeing themselves as constrained by current conditions to envisioning a fundamentally different future. They can break through the boundaries of their current thinking and discover future possibilities around which they can rally and to which they can commit inspired performance.

Most community colleges do not share a stated vision to which all those involved are committed and will devote their talents and energies. The executive leadership of most colleges has little experience in aligning all functions and development efforts toward achieving that vision. Many staff members are likely to question whether a vision statement is important and will have any relationship to their daily work. Given this set of circumstances, there also is no doubt that community college leaders do not yet fully know or sense the power of vision.

Leading a collegewide process of shared-vision development has more to do with who the leader is than what he or she does. There is a spiritual quality to the leader's role in such an endeavor. Successful college leaders are viewed as exemplifying the highest values toward which the college should strive. Not everyone will agree with the leader's vision, but they will feel that his or her "heart is in the right place." The vision work of the leader raises the sights of others and engages them in reexamining old assumptions and considering new ways of thinking.

At the heart of building a shared vision is the task of designing permanent processes through which people in every niche can speak from the heart about what really matters to them. The degree of openness and caring is especially important to the quality and power of the results. The content of a true shared vision cannot be dictated; it can only emerge from a coherent process of reflection and conversation (Senge, 1994c, pp. 299, 593).

Developing a shared vision requires a special set of leadership skills because it is a conceptual and creative process. The leader must provide an environment that enables all people involved to connect their visions of what they want the college to become to the visions of others. For many leaders, this role is dramatically different from the "ivory tower" role of the past. In the complex and rapidly changing world of the new century, the lone leader cannot possibly know everyone's vision. When each unit must be able to respond quickly and effectively to the changing needs of its customers, all college people must have an internalized beacon of institutional vision and values to guide daily decisions. The president cannot simply pronounce what the vision is; instead, each person must make a personal commitment in his or her heart and mind to a vision each was involved in creating. Senge (1990, p. 206) states:

> A shared vision is not an idea. It is not even an important idea such as freedom. It is, rather, a force in people's hearts, a force of impressive power. At its simplest level, a shared vision is the answer to the question, "What do we want to create?"

A vision is not just a target out there in the future. Seymour Eskow, speaking at a 1994 conference at Rockland Community College, New York, said:

> At all times in the history of man there have been major and minor prophets calling us to greatness. If we hear their calls, we respond first as individual men and women, lifting up our eyes and changing our minds and our hearts and our directions. Most of us also believe that history has taught us that uplifting the individual is not enough, that the prophet must find a priest to build a church, that the vision of the new faith will blur if it does not find a new form, that schools and courts and political parties and churches—all human institutions—are attempts to memorialize a vision, to house a dream, to be a response to a call to greatness.

For the community college, this prophesy-fulfilling process needs to be more fully defined. There are five interrelated processes that provide the pathway from mission and vision to the specific daily actions that channel people toward a preferred future. Examples from WCC are provided:

• The college **mission statement** is the most enduring and unchanging representation of the college's social purpose, functions, and values. It answers the question: Why do we exist?

WCC's mission statement declares: "WCC makes a positive difference in people's lives through accessible and excellent educational programs and services."

• A **shared vision statement** is co-created by all those who will carry it out. This is a brief and compelling outline of the future condition everyone will work together to achieve. It answers the question: What will we be in the future?

WCC's vision statement asserts: "We achieve student, community, and staff success. We work to increase student success through continuous improvement of our programs, services, processes, skills, and knowledge. We achieve excellence in teaching and learning, and all college functions are aligned to produce this result. All staff members are involved in continuously learning how to improve learning. We work in teams and help each other be successful."

• A **set of effectiveness indicators and measures** quantifies and verifies progress toward the achievement of mission and vision. An indicator might specify the targeted success level of students who transfer from the community college to a university, and the measures would provide the means of assessment. These answer the question: How will we know we are making progress toward achieving our goals?

Some WCC indicators measure whether students achieve their goals, which include job success, transfer success, and/or personal enrichment; students are satisfied with their WCC experience; WCC meets community workforce needs; and staff are proud of their work and satisfied with their work life.

• A **continuous improvement process** is designed to align all college functions and systems toward achieving the vision. This CQI process answers the question: How do we align all college functions and processes toward our goals?

WCC's SUCCESS System has four elements: plan, do, measure, and feedback. Each year the measurement of student, community, and staff success outcomes is the basis for planning institutional improvement and development.

• **Strategic and annual plans** specify tactics for closing the gap between the vision and actual performance. The plans answer the question: What specific steps will we take to achieve the vision, and how should we allocate staff time, funds, and other resources to maximize the leverage applied?

WCC's strategic goals, or outcomes of significance, include: continuously learning how to improve performance at each stage of the student's flow through college programs and services; creating a new "Open Door to Success" in cooperation with community partners; and designing a faster-paced instructional program development and improvement model to quickly meet rapidly changing educational needs of businesses and community groups.

Survey respondent Charles Spence, president of Florida Community College at Jacksonville, provided leadership in the process of developing a new shared vision which involved 800 staff members. Once the new statements were completed, a process known as "visual management" was implemented. This involves the campuswide display of banners, posters, and other attention-getting devices which highlight the new compact. These displays serve as constant visual reminders of the future that the staff is committed to creating. Roger Worsley, president of Laredo Community College, Texas, led "visioning workshops" that provided an environment for college staff to create a new vision statement. Humber College, Toronto, Ontario, identifies being in the "learning services business" as the key to its future, and has formed a Marketing Task Force to undertake a mission review and vision-creation process focusing on the emerging educational needs of community constituencies.

Jerry Moskus, president of Lane Community College, Oregon, states:

> I provided leadership in the development of a "vision of the future" statement that was a collaboration staff effort and approved by the College Council. The statement reads in part: "Lane Community College provides a quality learning experience in a caring environment."

The Lane vision statement is based on the common interests of quality and learning. The vision statement contains a set of unifying principles: respect for the individual, providing quality learning experiences, commitment to excellence, promoting a sense of achievement, ensuring a participatory environment, open communication, management with goals, connection with the community, and developing a sense of community ownership.

Charles Green, chancellor of Houston Community College District, Texas, states:

> The development of our vision started with Flight 2000, a forum at which 200 community and business leaders, board members, and staff came together to share their views about the future of HCCD. The vision was established and has been continuously reinforced through our publications and a yearly collegewide convocation for all staff members. As a result, we are undergoing a true transformation based on shared vision.

A good example is HCCD's Project Future Perfect. Green states:

> Our leadership training program is unique in that the participants come from all areas of the college and from faculty, administration, and support staff. Twenty participants annually receive a yearlong experience designed to increase

their knowledge of the "big picture" and improve their leadership skills in whatever capacity they function.

John Anthony, president of Collin County Community College, Texas, states, "We have had almost total involvement of faculty and staff in the creation of a vision for the district. This has been brought about through master planning workshops, councils, and committees."

John Blong, chancellor of Eastern Iowa Community College District, states that the college "spent a period of 20 months developing a shared vision among all constituencies of the college. Along with this shared vision, we have established an environmental scanning system that allows EICCD to not only be able to react to our environment but hopefully anticipate our community's needs."

James Linksz of Bucks County Community College, Pennsylvania, formed a planning task force made up of representatives of all constituency groups. The task force developed a vision statement, which states that the college "will excel in providing high quality, accessible higher education to the citizens of Bucks County.... We will be self-renewing, committed to continuous institutional assessment to measure our success and responsiveness."

Walter Bumphus, president of Brookhaven College, Texas, states:

> Aligning the college toward a shared vision is among the top priorities of the president. Every meeting, every committee, every document, and every action must be viewed as an opportunity to communicate the vision and align the college to it. As an example, we constantly strive to remove barriers, inconveniences, and frustrations that negatively effect student success.

There is power in a shared vision—power that can shape community colleges for the new century. To test this, it is important to compare the impact a personal vision can have on an individual life to the impact a shared vision can have on a community college.

When people have a clear vision of something they want, they often act in extraordinary ways to achieve it. A strong commitment to a personal vision is a powerful force that guides or even compels them toward the desired result. Anyone who has worked on a graduate degree while holding a full-time job and raising a family knows this power. The promise of an advanced degree and the professional opportunities it may offer compels the individual to study for untold hours while others engage in more "normal" activities.

This uniquely human capacity to leap into the unknown future and actually "see" an outcome that has not yet been realized has a magical quality. Through visioning, people see beyond the problems and routines of the day to a preferred state which they can create. As people imagine this preferred state, the vision becomes very real. They go through a conceptual process of testing and sorting options as the vision evolves to its final form. Then one day everything clicks into place—they have in their mind a compelling vision, often with key ideas about how to make it real. Its power drives them to give up cherished habits or reorganize their schedules. Family, friends, and associates may notice that they have reached a defining moment in their lives and that their behavior has changed accordingly.

If a personal vision can have such power, how might this quality be transferred to community colleges? It is very desirable that all those involved with a college share a vision of the college's future. A shared institutional vision imprinted in everyone's minds also can serve as a beacon to guide daily decisions. This unity of purpose and of motion is the basis for creating an effective community college.

Senge (1994c, pp. 300, 593) states that the shared-vision discipline focuses on building shared meaning—a collective sense of what is important, and why. It is a discipline to be engaged in by all units of the college, not just by the college as a whole. This opportunity to actively consider what vision has real meaning for them, rather than to have the vision passed down from top management, can dramatically increase the staff engagement:

> Having gone through the frustration and ultimate satisfaction of creating a personal vision and a shared vision for their immediate team, they become more devoted to building shared vision and shared meaning for the entire organization. Team members will often suggest joint sessions with other teams to share visions and develop action plans that they can implement together. As that process is repeated among many teams and multiple pairings, the whole organization is engaged and enriched, and multiple strands of shared meaning begin to bind the organization together.

There has been great variation in the progress of community colleges toward establishing shared meaning and vision at all levels. Senge outlines a very useful set of developmental stages to help determine the progress of top management in learning to listen more, and of the staff in developing their leadership capabilities in the progression toward a shared vision.

Stage One: Telling. Top leadership tells the staff what the vision is.

A "told" vision is still a vision, and can have power in galvanizing action. However, it is important to keep in mind that staff are passive recipients of the vision so they are less likely to fully commit themselves. The telling stage can be very effective during times of crisis.

Stage Two: Selling. Top leadership attempts to enroll staff in the vision.

Leaders make it clear that the vision can be achieved only if the staff is on board. The message is that the leader is depending on the staff, and that the staff has influence. However, compliance rather than commitment is still a real option for staff members.

Stage Three: Testing. Top leadership sends drafts of the vision statement to the staff for refinement and redesign.

By modifying the final statement based on which parts the staff accept and which really matter to them, it is likely to generate more support and commitment than one developed at the telling or selling stages.

Stage Four: Consulting. Top leadership develops the vision statement through dialogue with staff groups.

Unlike the earlier stages, top leadership does not begin with a draft vision statement. Rather, ideas come forward from staff groups with boundaries or guidelines prepared by top leadership. It is the task of the leadership to capture key vision themes from the staff without ending up with an all-things-to-all-people statement. Because the staff have been involved in the process from the beginning, and may review drafts based on their suggestions, the likelihood of shared commitment increases.

Stage Five: Co-creating. All staff members are involved in creating the vision statement.

This process permits staff to give voice to how their personal visions link to the vision of their unit and to that of the college as a whole. What is likely to emerge is a statement of common aspirations to which all can commit. Since staff from all areas of the college have been involved, the vision statement should be able to capture a strong sense of alignment between unit visions and the vision of the whole institution.

The leadership challenge is to guide the development and implementation of a vision that has wide appeal and becomes ingrained in everyone's forward strivings and active aspirations. Fred Polak (1961, p. 43) defined images of the future as condensed and crystallized expectations prevailing among the people. Speaking of earlier images of the future, he said:

> These images of the future not only reflected the shape of things to come in the present, but they gave shape to those things and their very becoming. The images of the future and their prophets were writing the history of the future—they made history by creating the future and by fulfilling their own prophesies. They were like powerful time bombs, exploding in the future, releasing a mighty stream of energy

flowing back to the present, which then pushed and pulled them to that future.

CHAPTER 6

The Spiritual Dimension of Leadership

"To value oneself and, at the same time, subordinate oneself to higher purposes and principles is the paradoxical essence of highest humanity and the foundation for leadership" (Stephen R. Covey, 1991, pp. 18-19).

I t may seem a bit strange to suggest that there is a spiritual dimension to community college leadership. People may be uncomfortable with the word "spiritual" because it suggests some involvement with organized religion, although that is not the meaning intended here. Community college leadership may be viewed as a set of management principles and techniques rather than spiritual principles. But this chapter introduces the concept that a leader's personal spiritual journey is the foundation for all of his or her leadership behavior. Hopefully, any reactions of strangeness and discomfort can be replaced with those of recognition and affirmation.

Everyone is a spiritual being in that each responds to transcendent, though not necessarily religious, values. Each person is on a spiritual journey of self-discovery and growth, and each holds a set of values and beliefs that transcends his or her own life to encompass the lives of others. For example, when people seek to serve others, they express their spiritual dimension, and when they advocate the open door and concern for those from all walks of life they show faith in an idea that will endure far beyond their own lifetimes. When people express their spiritual dimension, they participate in a process that has lifted and enabled every effective society and organization. Covey (1991, p. 18) writes of "inviolate principles"—natural laws in the human dimension that are woven into the fabric of every society and constitute the roots of every organization that has endured and prospered:

> Principles are not invented by us or by society; they are the laws of the universe that pertain to human relationships and human organizations. They are part of the human condition, consciousness, and conscience. To the degree that people recognize and live in harmony with such basic principles as fairness, equity, justice, integrity, honesty, and trust, they

move toward either survival and stability on the one hand or disintegration and destruction on the other.

The spiritual dimension of leadership is defined here as personal and transcendent convictions that guide daily leadership conduct. These deeply held ideals drive leadership behavior. They can be discussed in two categories: those that inform personal values and beliefs, and those that inform perceptions and actions regarding the value and importance of community colleges.

LEADING FROM WITHIN

The movie *Chariots of Fire* gives us the words, "From where does the courage come to run the race to the end? From within." Dag Hammarskjold, a beloved United Nations secretary general, said, "The longest journey is the journey within." A personal spiritual journey is the inner process of discovering and surrendering to a set of higher purposes and principles that transcends mere existence and individual human needs and tendencies. On this journey, one learns to release and display true essence in the forms of love, joy, hope, awe, wonder, imagination, good will, and trust. The degree to which one expresses these becomes the most fundamental determinant of the effectiveness of leadership.

It often seems difficult for people to show their true spiritual essence, and this may be particularly true for leaders. When making decisions, leaders listen to inner voices of doubt, anxiety, fear of failure, and fear of embarrassment, as well as those of love, joy, and hope. This journey is one of learning to listen more to the uplifting voices more than to the caveats of human frailty.

> It is hard to change habits, develop virtues, learn basic disciplines, keep promises, be faithful to vows, exercise courage, or be genuinely considerate of the feelings and convictions of others. Nonetheless, it's the true test and manifestation of our maturity. To value oneself and, at the same time, subordinate oneself to higher purposes and principles is the paradoxical essence of highest humanity and the foundation for leadership (Covey, 1991, pp. 18-19).

Max DePree (1989, p. 15) put it more simply:

> Leaders owe a certain maturity. Maturity is expressed in a sense of self-worth, a sense of belonging, a sense of expectancy, a sense of responsibility, a sense of accountability, and a sense of equality.

Everyone is involved in the lifelong process of becoming. As people experience the joys and trials of life, they are on Covey's "upward spiral" of living, loving, learning, and leaving a legacy. And, regardless of religious convictions, this personal journey has a spiritual dimension. Deep within everyone is a conviction that life has purpose, meaning, and direction higher than mere existence.

At a recent leadership retreat, participants studied the personal journeys of heroes in medieval myths, and then reflected these same elements into their personal lives. Each hero would experience some form of separation from his or her current situation, enter a period of trial and failure which tested courage and intelligence, achieve the quest (although in the form of deeper understanding rather than the gold or other material gain expected at the outset), then return from the journey as a changed person. The participants could identify with such universal and timeless themes in their own lives. Chuck Lofy (1993, p. 15) writes:

> We are moved to tears, laughter, awe, anger, and resolve by how the hero, our surrogate, handles them. We recognize them in our bones as a metaphor of the journey each of us makes through the world from cradle to grave.

The rhythms of a person's life are inexorably tied to the rhythms of his or her leadership behavior. James M. Kouzes and Barry Z. Posner conduct periodic surveys of employees to determine what values, characteristics, and personal traits they look for in supervisors. Employees most want leaders who are credible and believable:

> What we found unexpectedly in our initial research and have reaffirmed ever since is that, above all else, people want leaders who are credible. We want to believe in our leaders. We want to have faith and confidence in them as people. We want to believe that their word can be trusted, that they have the knowledge and skill to lead, and that they are personally excited and enthusiastic about the direction in which they are headed. Credibility is the foundation of leadership (Kouzes and Posner, 1993, p. 22).

Lawrence Tyree, president of Santa Fe Community College, Florida, states in his survey response:

> My leadership style has always been based on trust and collaboration. Such a style tends to motivate faculty, staff, and students because they realize that they are truly valued as

members of the institution and that they have a genuine stake in the college's current and future success. The keys to such a style are giving people a chance to be involved and respecting their involvement even when it would be easier not to.

There are times when every leader believes he or she acted too quickly in an interaction with a staff member, and then experienced regret at having responded with anger, suspicion, doubt, or fear. In such cases, there is a desire to have paused to listen to the inner spiritual voice advising patience. Covey (1994, p. 281) writes:

> We see how vital it is to pause in that space between stimulus and response so that we can listen to our conscience and exercise the attributes of the heart to make the best choices. We see that there are purposes higher than self toward which we can focus our energies and effort.

Perhaps William Henry Channing said it best:

> In a word, to let the
> spiritual, unbidden and
> unconscious, grow up
> through the commonplace.

EXPRESSING THE COLLEGE'S SPIRITUAL DIMENSION

The community college is founded on a great and powerful idea—that talent and ambition are very widely distributed in society, and accessible and excellent education is a path to individual and community growth and achievement. The community college is "democracy's college" in the local community. When Robert Greenleaf (1978) used the term "servant leadership," he meant that the leader is the servant of a great idea:

> If the dream has the quality of greatness, it not only provides the overarching vision for the undertaking; it also penetrates deeply into the psyches of all who are drawn to it and savor its beauty, its rightness, and its wisdom. The test of greatness in a dream is that it has the energy to lift people out of their moribund ways to a level of being and relat-

ing to the future that can be faced with more hope than most of us can summon today.

Only when one has a powerful passion for the mission and meaning of the community college and a love for the people who are served can he or she be an effective community college leader.

The effective community college leader has a strong sense of stewardship for the community college idea. That leader advocates and facilitates it. WCC's local community refers to it as "the miracle in the apple orchard" because the main campus is located on the former site of such an orchard. This is an apt image since miracles do happen every day at community colleges throughout the country. The miracles are not attractive buildings or great programs, but what occurs in the hearts and minds of community college staff—the faith that students can overcome major personal hurdles to achieve personal success. The conviction that people from all backgrounds can grow and achieve is the foundation of community colleges' daily actions and distinguishes them among higher educational institutions.

Carl Rolvaag, a Minnesotan who wrote a chronology of the Norwegian pioneers' journey from the old country to the cold, forbidding plains of Minnesota and South Dakota, said they "attempted the impossible and achieved the unbelievable." They were miracle workers because they believed so fervently in the American dream that they attempted far more than common sense or good judgment would suggest. The miracle was fundamentally in their hearts and minds; what actually happened as they braved the hardships of establishing life in a new country was an expression of that miracle.

There is a parallel here for community college leaders. They believe so fervently that people can overcome hurdles to achieve personal growth through education that they are undeterred by conventional wisdom or even fairly obvious evidence to the contrary. And the success of students who become a part of this spirit is an expression of that miracle.

An old saying has it that "every age needs its prophets and its carpenters." Prophets are needed to broaden horizons and challenge society to think beyond its own circumstances and lifetime. Among them are this country's founders, who dreamed of a nation based on principles of opportunity, freedom, equality, and justice. In a small way, community college leaders must also serve as prophets. They must articulate the principles that make colleges instruments for reaching the American dream for all groups, including those that have been systematically excluded from access to the economic mainstream. At the same time, every age needs its carpenters—those who give shape and substance to the dream. Community college people are the carpenters; they give shape and substance to "democracy's college" in communities across the land.

Leaders have an obligation to students, staff, and communities to participate with them in creating a culture based on universal values. Senge (1994b, p.11) writes that "a learning organization must be grounded in a culture based on the transcendent values of love, wonder, humility, and compassion."

The nurturing of an organization that is continuously learning how to express these transcendent values captures the essence of what community college leadership must do in preparing for the new century. The image of the leader having a "covenant" with the people who make up the organization has much appeal in this regard.

> Leaders owe a covenant to the corporation or institution, which is, after all, a group of people. Leaders owe the organization a new reference point for what caring, purposeful, committed people can be in the institutional setting. Notice that I did not say what people can do—what we can do is merely a consequence of what we can be. Corporations, like the people who compose them, are always in a state of becoming. Covenants bind people together and enable them to meet their corporate needs by meeting the needs of one another (DePree, 1989, p. 16).

CHAPTER 7

Learning to Improve Learning

"Learning does not mean acquiring more information, but expanding the ability to produce the results we truly want in life. It is lifelong generative learning. And learning organizations are not possible unless they have people at every level who practice it" (Peter Senge, 1990, p. 142).

Community college leadership in the new century will be learner-based. It will empower student, community, and staff learning. Everyone involved with the college, including the president, will learn continuously how to improve learning. It will increase student and community learning by constantly improving college programs, services, processes, and staff skills and knowledge. This chapter addresses the ways learner-based leadership will create the self-evaluating and self-generating community college of the future.

Discussion of a learner-based future requires reflection on its foundation. In preparing for the future, past achievements sometimes go unrecognized. Ernest Boyer has often reminded his audiences that the leader must honor the future and the past. It is from this authentic blending of memory and vision, he contends, that the campus finds its pulse. Even as a community college shapes the future, it recalls its roots and affirms the convictions that led to its creation.

"Continuous learning" in the community college should be defined at the outset. Senge (1990, p. 3) describes a learning organization as a place in which people continually expand their capacity to create the results they truly desire, where expansive patterns of thinking are nurtured, where collective aspiration is set free, and where people are continuously learning how to learn together.

During most of community college history, it was assumed that presidents could do the learning for whole organizations. They could sense the changes in the external and internal environments and articulate changes in their colleges' goals. To some extent, the slow pace of change and the relative predictability of events actually made this possible.

Today, about the only certainty is that the unexpected will occur. Change occurs so rapidly and constantly that everyone in the organization must learn. They must connect what they see in the environment to what they do. All staff must continuously increase their capacity through individual learning and participation in organizational learning. No one person can see for the whole organization, so everyone must see the connection between changes in their work and the future of the whole organization.

Thinking about increased staff empowerment, seeing the organization as an open learning system, and viewing the organization as more than the sum of its parts underlie any learning-organization concept. These ideas represent new knowledge about how organizations and the world work. In the mid-1990s, community college leaders have access to new knowledge from a variety of disciplines that will have a profound impact on how the community college of the future is designed. The task is to synthesize and apply this knowledge to reshape the community college mission for the turbulent and uncertain new century.

A number of community colleges are using CQI and learning-organization concepts to create an environment of empowerment and continuous learning. William Wenrich, chancellor of the Dallas County Community College District, Texas, provides leadership to create a quality center as part of the district service center. Over 200 district leaders have been trained in CQI processes through the Leadership DCCCD program, and the new employee orientation program emphasizes high-quality service to students and other groups. The district's purpose statement says: "We strive to meet the needs and exceed the expectations of those whom we serve." Wenrich recognizes the importance of empowerment when he states, "My philosophy is to employ quality people, empower them to do their job by removing barriers and getting out of their way."

Marvin Lane, president of Lamar Community College, Colorado, states:

> I now try to consider the total organization as a facilitator of learning. Most recently, my college has completed a strategic plan entitled "A Culture for Learning." It is my goal to develop a "learning culture" for our campus. It is my hope that LCC can specifically target campus resources to facilitate student, individual employee, team, and organizational learning.

Norm Nielson, president of Kirkwood Community College, Iowa, in describing the use of student-outcome data to guide continuous improvement, states:

> We are establishing an entirely new set of criteria to measure student outcomes based on a variety of measurements. In addition, we are part of an ongoing League for Innovation project in benchmarking, especially in areas related to finance.

Roger Van Winkle, president of Massachusetts Bay Community College, describes feedback processes in its CQI program:

> Focus groups have been employed by the college to provide feedback from various constituencies. Those included in these groups are mature women, recent high school graduates, dislocated workers, single parents, older males, and business and industrial customers.

John Blong of Eastern Iowa states:

> Eastern Iowa Community College District has become committed to continuous quality improvement. As a part of that commitment, every full-time employee has had a minimum of 24 hours of training to help them better serve their customers.

Van Winkle states:

> Community colleges, more than any other educational institution, must change or die. If we become "just another institution" offering two-year programs instead of four-year programs, we bring nothing to the educational table. The dynamic force of the community college is centered in its ability to change, adapt, and renew the evolving educational needs of those it serves.

Community college practitioners are the translators of new knowledge emerging from fields of study such as organizational development, general systems theory, quantum physics, biology, and complexity or chaos theory. The core ideas to be derived from these fields that have applicability to the community college of the new century can be summarized as follows:

- Human systems are open learning systems that can adapt to a changing context in ways that are similar to natural ones. Community colleges can be viewed as an organism that can learn and improve as a whole. Older approaches to organizational development focused on breaking down the organization into its parts for manageability and control. Emerging approaches focus more on the alignment of all parts of the organization toward a shared mission and vision.

• The old hierarchical management style is giving way to a horizontal style. The old restricted power and knowledge to a few and the new distributes power and knowledge to many. This shift is based on the assumption that staff members, given the power, knowledge, and resources they need, will be more creative, productive, and accountable than if they are tightly controlled.

• The community college can organize or regenerate based on feedback from its environment with the result that it will achieve greater integration and wholeness.

   All units of the college form an interlocking whole. The college in turn is nested within a constantly interacting community learning system.

The seminal idea that emerges from this new knowledge and which has applicability to the community college is that all natural and human systems have a direction in which they will naturally move. For example, a garden is a system that will naturally follow the laws of nature. A gardener may impose his or her rules (plant in rows, remove weeds, etc.), but left unattended the garden will quickly reimpose the laws of nature. In a similar fashion the community college is a human system founded on a central mission or purpose toward which those involved will be naturally drawn. The single most important role of the leader in this new world view is to create a design and an environment for continuous learning and adaptation.

Based on the four core ideas listed previously, the following is a design for the continuous learning and adaptation of the community college:

• **Student learning**. The ultimate purpose of the learning community college is to increase student learning. The alignment of all college functions to support teaching and learning and student success is a key objective of the learning community college.

• **Community learning**. The community college is an integral part of the community learning system. The college can be a catalyst for bringing together various sectors to promote community building and to address problems. All educational institutions in the community may also be viewed as a learning community. The new century campus should be based on bringing all of the existing campuses conceptually together in a coordinated web. For example, those agencies involved in workforce development or services to all income groups can become a learning system wherein the whole accomplishes more than the separate parts.

- **Staff learning at the organizational level.** This will occur through the continuous improvement of programs, services, processes, and staff skills. Measuring the outcomes of student learning—such as job placement, career advancement, or university transfer—using the measurement data to plan improvements, and taking actions to make specific improvements on an ongoing basis becomes the CQI cycle of the college.

  Much organizational learning occurs through cross-functional teams. When staff members representing different sectors of the college come together, much of the learning that occurs involves mutual discovery of ways to improve relationships among them.

- **Staff learning at the individual level.** Staff learning must go beyond the traditional professional development activities that take place at most community colleges. The starting point is leadership's intention to create an environment for personal growth by each staff member. The personal vision of the staff member is given expression within the organization. What individuals regard as truly important is taken into account in establishing the college's priorities for change. The idea that the organization must reconcile the needs of the individual staff member to the needs of the whole college is not familiar to most community colleges. Yet individual continuous learning depends on clarifying what is important (personal vision) and seeing the gap between the vision and reality. Senge (1990, p. 142) suggests that this "creative tension" between vision and reality provides the impetus for continuous improvement:

  > The juxtaposition of vision (what we want) and a clear picture of current reality (where we are relative to what we want) generates what we call "creative tension." Learning does not mean acquiring more information, but expanding the ability to produce the results we truly want in life. It is lifelong generative learning. And learning organizations are not possible unless they have people at every level who practice it.

Community college presidents and other leaders can be role models by having personal visions that provide beacons for daily actions. When people sort out the big rocks in their lives from the gravel and sand, they are more likely to find the focus and balance necessary for effective leadership. And when they honor the personal visions of other staff members, they create an environment for self-actualization of all staff as individuals and the continuous propulsion of the col-

lege toward its vision. The organization and the individuals in it become generative and adaptive.

CHAPTER 8

Designing the Organization of the New Century

"In short, the organization chart doesn't show what we do, for whom we do it, or how we do it. Other than that, it's a great picture of a business" (Geary Rummler, 1990, p. 5).

There is little room for debate: today's community colleges are organized as bureaucracies. They learned bureaucratic skills well from their parents, Father University and Mother High School. They have roughly the same specialized subcultures or disciplines and the same divisions between the faculty and administration as universities. Their rigid top-down structure is similar to the traditional public school's, with each function in its appropriate box: the finance box, the personnel box, the instruction and student services boxes, and so on. Staff members are taught to operate within their boxes and report through channels. This is the organizational paradigm they inherited, and they have learned their lessons well and made their parents proud. But community colleges, along with other organizations, are learning that this paradigm is inadequate for the demands of the new century.

If community college managers were asked to draw pictures of their organizations, almost certainly they would sketch boxes and lines that show the hierarchical patterns of the college. The units of the management structure would be connected by vertical reporting relations. What would be wrong with this picture? Geary Rummler, an organizational design consultant, shares this answer:

> It doesn't show the products or services we provide. It leaves out the customers we serve. And it makes no sense of the work flow through which we develop, produce, and deliver our products. In short, the organization chart doesn't show what we do, for whom we do it, or how we do it. Other than that, it's a great picture of a business (Rummler, 1990, p. 5).

The traditional organization chart of the community college serves a limited purpose in showing how managers are grouped by function and to whom they report. It tells how college management is organized but not how the college is organized. There is a big difference. The organizational design of the college as a whole includes the way it has arranged structures, processes, and assignments to carry out its goals.

Organizational design includes the vertical or administrative structure, but places emphasis on the horizontal dimensions of the work structure, most commonly described as "process management." Instead of viewing the college through the lens of their own functions, managers shift to view their work through the lens of key cross-functional processes. The focus changes from managing "inside the boxes" of the administrative structure to managing "in the white space" between the boxes (Rummler, 1990). Process management assumes that most gains in customer service will come from improving the critical interfaces between these boxes.

How does process management apply to community colleges? This question can be answered by examining their typical organizational design, considering why changes are needed, and exploring what the new century's design might look like.

The typical college has management "silos": instruction, student services, finance, human resources, community relations, information systems, institutional research, and so on. For each of these there is a leader who advocates for the function, seeks its success, and protects its interests. Unit staff report up to the leader, who then interacts with leaders at the top of other silos. Communications with other silos take the form of messages thrown over the wall into the next silo in the work flow. Success is measured by the individual success of each silo.

What is wrong with the vertical organizational design described above? Why is change needed?

There is too much remanagement. Each person in the silo passes work up the administrative chain and, to some extent, supervisors redo the work, wasting time and energy and underusing staff members' talents. Staff may feel like drones who pass their products on to those who do the really important work. Much work that could be done across units at lower levels moves up to await the attention of those at higher levels. Staff members do not feel empowered to use creativity or initiative.

Communication with other units is stifled. Staff have more incentive to communicate within their silo than with people in other units. There may even be sanctions within the unit that discourage cross-functional communication. Issues that need quick responses pile up at the top even though they could be resolved through cross-functional communication at lower levels.

Success of the unit is emphasized over that of other units. Institutional procedures such as administrative evaluation and salary determination often focus on individual rather than team or institutional achievement. Managers may be recognized and rewarded for the success of their unit rather than that of other units that depend on their work flow.

Units are not aligned to the vision, mission, and goals of the whole college. Staff members may not visualize the college as a system, seeing it instead as a collection of units each pursuing its own ends within a vague sense of common purpose. There may not be a strong sense within the unit of how its work contributes to the institution. A lack of shared vision for the college among staff members may lead to greater focus on individual units' goals.

In response to these problems, fundamental change is taking place in community colleges' organizational design. To explore some dimensions of the organizational design of the new century, imagine a horizontal rather than vertical emphasis. A beginning point might be to think about the key processes that will drive this cross-functional design. Then imagine college leaders serving as advocates and sponsors for improvement of these key processes in much the same way they now serve their own silos.

The key cross-functional processes of community colleges that will drive the achievement of its mission may vary from college to college, but the following list provides examples:

- Student progress (the stages of the student's flow through college services and programs)
- Master class schedule (the process that determines the time, length, and place of college offerings each semester or term)
- Annual planning and budgeting
- Staff success (recruitment, orientation, professional development, and evaluation)
- Student registration
- Community success (involvement in community development and leadership activities)
- Administrative support (administrative systems such as staff hiring, purchasing, program promotion, and publications)
- Instructional program development and improvement
- Instructional and classroom support (learning resources, teaching and learning support, educational services, and curriculum development support)
- Board of trustees policy and executive guidelines

Some elements that would shift the college from the current vertical perspective to the horizontal perspective of the new century could include:

- **A steering committee or leadership team made up of representatives of all staff groups.** This steering committee works with the president and governing board to establish the strategic directions and the annual action plans of the college. It also serves as the steering committee for involving all staff groups in cross-functional teams and single-task action teams.

- **Cross-functional staff teams focused on key processes.** At some colleges, the steering committee might create only two or three cross-functional teams during a given year in recognition of limited staff time and energy, while other colleges may have teams working on a number of key processes. Each team concentrates on a single process. It will be responsible for continuous improvement in the process based on feedback data from those being served. Since each process is made up of subprocesses, the team is likely to select only portions of the overall process for improvement during a given year.

A complex cross-functional process requires continuous long-term improvement, and the teams usually are regarded as permanent groups. An important feature of a team is the involvement of a college executive who serves as the group's sponsor. The executive advocates and coaches the team rather than supervising it. The primary objective is to have the executive focus on relationship building between the units involved in the process.

Cross-functional teams are likely to function on a permanent basis since key processes will always need updating and improvement. Single-action teams are also made up of members from various college functions and staff groups (and sometimes student and community representatives as well), but they address specific problems or improvement needs and then disband. Single-task action teams may serve at the office, departmental, divisional, or institutional level. The teams may be formed by the steering committee, or they may "bubble up" from needs identified at other levels. These short-term, nimble, and flexible teams complement the more permanent cross-functional teams and complete the horizontal continuous improvement structure.

CHAPTER 9

Staying Student- and Community-Centered

"Make sure that the good produced by your college exceeds the cost of the college, and remember that your college exists to make certain that the lives of your students and the well-being of your community are better because of you" (John Carver, 1993).

CUSTOMER-DRIVEN LEADERSHIP

To some of America's educators it seems absurd, almost sacrilegious, to suggest that public educational systems need to be reinvented. "After all," one is apt to hear, "this country's strength has been undergirded by its mass education system. Indeed, it has prospered for nearly two hundred years with more or less the same system of educational administration and delivery. It's not that schools need to change; students and communities need to recognize that we are the professionals and we know what's best for them." Although the argument may be a bit contrived, it harbors the substance of truth.

The American public has developed, mostly in the past twenty years, the core perception that schools and colleges should be serving students and their communities as customers. The traditional notion that education is immune from serious scrutiny has largely disappeared. Louis Gerstner, Jr. (1994, pp. 1, 2), chairman and chief executive officer of IBM Corporation, summarizes the current public frustration with public education by stating that economic vitality is the product of unending change, but public education has not gone through any revitalizing change. He further asserts that the nation's public schools are "hopelessly out of sync with the realities of modern economic, social, and political life. They are a bureaucratic monopoly which cannot last." He continues to develop a compelling argument by citing the twenty-fourth annual Gallup poll of attitudes toward public schools, which found that half of Americans now support private-school vouchers. Gerstner's comments were primarily directed at the K–12 system, but the principle is the same. The American public expects accountable, relevant, and convenient educational services. Community colleges should recognize this fundamental and permanent shift in public attitude and avoid slipping into the complacency that plagues so many of our public schools.

Russell Edgerton, president of the American Association for Higher Education, underscores the same call for change (1994, pp. 1, 2). As the pressures of the twenty-first century emerge, Edgerton summarizes public sentiment by asking, "Where the hell is higher education?" He postulates that higher education (meaning universities) must "let go of the traditional academic conception of 'service' as in 'teaching, research, and service.'" He suggests that all critical tasks performed by universities must change if they are truly to connect with the needs of the larger community. Community colleges, although traditionally needs-based and market-driven, must ever remain alert and customer-focused if they hope to remain architects of a healthy and prosperous America. Ignoring this demand for better services will be a failure in their mission as community-based organizations and deserve the same criticism currently leveled at public schools and universities.

Anyone who works in a community college should embrace what John Carver promoted when speaking to governing board trustees in a 1993 address: "Make sure that the good produced by your college exceeds the cost of the college, and remember that your college exists to make certain that the lives of your students and the well-being of your community are better because of you."

Central Piedmont Community College, North Carolina, has adopted two litmus-test questions that capture the essence of Carver's admonition: Is it good for the students, and is it good for the community? The challenge for the community college movement is to keep moving to meet the emerging needs of its customers: students and communities. Inevitably, the question of leadership must be addressed by everyone.

By now everyone in community college administration is aware of the demands for new leadership styles. The traditional benevolent-autocrat or paternalistic model has become ineffective, and some movement toward participatory models has occurred at most colleges. Many colleges have successfully emulated leadership models adopted by business. The rekindled interest in CQI on shop floors is making a fairly good transition to community colleges. But not all college climates are receptive to new leadership, and not all leaders are receptive to changing their styles. As flower production requires the proper preparation of the flower bed, so too must colleges be prepared for change. The big question is: Which leadership style is best?

Volumes have been written on the subject of leadership, and each makes a persuasive case for the styles preferred by its author. However, there never will be a perfect leadership style for any organization. Organizations are dynamic, reflecting the collective personality and societal needs of their time. Yet each new book on leadership that has a new wrinkle or seems to better address current issues, becomes instantly popular. Everyone is seeking better ways to influence human behavior, meet customers' needs, and fulfill stated missions. The demands on community colleges seem to be accelerating and many fear that traditional processes will be so all-consuming that real service—meaningful results to students and communities—will vanish.

Noted educational leader and author James L. Fisher (1994) makes an airtight case for transformational leadership, asserting that only strong presidents, not committees, can be expected to bring about any significant change to a college. Madeleine F. Green (1994), a vice president for the American Council on Education, makes an equally compelling case for an interactive leadership style which engages the entire college community, through relationship building, to mobilize toward common goals. Both authors are right. Although their leadership preferences diverge, there is no doubt that both styles can be effective given the proper circumstances.

Margaret J. Wheatley (1992) compares the idea of relationships and connectedness to nature. In quantum physics, the notion that order inevitably comes from chaos seems applicable to organizational development and its leadership model. She suggests that scientists once studied systems by focusing on whole structures, which led them away from observing the processes of change and growth that make a cohesive system over time. The upshot is that any organization should also look to its parts (its people) to understand and influence the whole organization. If leaders of an organization hope to keep order and move forward, they should concentrate on the relationships of people, departments, customers, and the environment at that specific point in its evolution.

These are three of the most popular models for leadership to propel community colleges into the new century as responsive and responsible public organizations. Fisher offers a successful, visionary leadership style based on applied practice. Green stresses the need for participatory and shared leadership as the wave of the future. And Wheatley suggests that relationships and their connectedness to each other will ultimately drive the evolution of organizational order and meaningfulness if leaders develop open climates. There is at least one more equally compelling style that should be considered. It comes not from an educator, but from an expert in organizational change: Stephen R. Covey.

Covey has put together the milestone book *Principle-Centered Leadership* (1992). It focuses primarily on corporate organizations, but its precepts are equally transferrable to community colleges. Covey asserts that ultimately a leader's character drives his or her leadership style. Whatever leaders have at the center of their lives affects their perceptions of everything around them. Therefore good leadership, in whatever setting, begins with the development of solid personal values and trust in others. As leaders mature, follow a code of values, and become trustworthy, their ability to lead expands. All leaders must have a solid personal foundation to be successful in the long term. Community college leaders must "walk the walk," and walk it consistently, before expecting others to follow.

Regardless of which style or combination of styles leaders consciously attempt to practice, they should:

• Establish a personal code of ethics
• Recognize that personal values must be harmonious with those of the college
• Establish and commit to a shared vision of what colleges can become
• Constantly build trust with all of constituents
• Recognize the necessity of situational leadership without compromising convictions
• Recognize that communities and colleges are dynamic and continuously evolving
• Recognize that building relationships never ends
• Understand that keeping open communication is vital
• Recognize that becoming customer-focused is paramount
• Realize that not everyone will appreciate them

STAYING STUDENT-CENTERED

Leading a college in an ever-changing environment is dangerous and rewarding. The challenge is to progress despite restrictive processes and provide more flexible services while holding fast to teaching excellence. Leaders will be able to meet the challenges of the new century if they remain committed to their primary customers: students. Further, they must totally commit to meeting student needs rather than to expecting students to conform to existing processes and traditions.

Changing Student Profiles

For many years the average age of the typical community college student has risen. Colleges adjusted by reaching out to adult students, understanding their unique needs, and providing classes that better met their schedules. Then research departments discovered that student body demographics were changing in more ways than age. Indeed, the whole student profile has changed rapidly, especially during the past decade.

Today's typical student body mirrors the changing populations being served. Colleges are serving recent high school graduates, young adults, the middle-aged, and senior citizens all in the same classroom. They represent the rich, the poor, and the middle class. They are becoming more ethnically and culturally diverse. For example, Central Piedmont serves some sixty thousand students annually. One hundred and seven foreign countries are represented in its classrooms, and CPCC is increasing its numbers of female, minority, and single-parent students. Obviously, the general public recognizes that education and skills development are imperative to self-sufficiency and that community colleges offer the best opportunity for most people. In short, community colleges have been discovered in a huge way. Now they're struggling to meet the new demands that accompany their new students.

Emerging Needs

It once was fairly easy to describe the educational services provided by community colleges: terminal technical degrees and transfer degrees. As student profiles changed, available services expanded. In some cases the college's identity blurred because of intense demands. It is no longer easy to describe all the services of community colleges without confusing the general public. Yet the fundamental purpose—to provide easy access to education and meet the needs of students and communities—has not changed. Some colleges are criticized by the media for chasing students to increase their budgets! Community colleges have sacrificed their traditional marketing identities by doing their jobs well. Marketing departments, like instructors and other staff members, will have to adjust to the new customers and capitalize on the value of expanded services as an extension of the original purpose. It won't be easy to explain to the public what community colleges have become and why they are so vital to their community's health if they attempt to "shotgun" market all of their services. It will be much more effective to "rifle" home the access issue and human development benefits for all residents who need educational services. A targeted approach to each market (e.g., workforce development, international students, senior citizens, literacy students, or technical and transfer students) would still be important, but the basic image should reflect the broader scope of the college's mission.

To explain these emerging services is one thing; to provide them effectively is quite another. In the sixties and seventies, most community college student bodies taking comprehensive curricula consisted of around thirty percent transfer students and seventy percent technical-occupational students. An additional group of continuing education students existed but was factored into the student mix as separate and unequal. Today the student bodies are twenty-five percent transfer students, fifty percent technical-occupational degree seekers, and twenty-five percent workers seeking skill upgrades. The line between credit and noncredit corporate students has all but collapsed as student needs have changed. Even degree completion is meaningless to most workers.

Colleges astute enough to continue embracing educational access as their fundamental mission are seizing this opportunity to serve a new sector of society. They recognize the need to merge corporate education with traditional curriculum instruction and are creating collaborative ways to accomplish it. Of course most noncredit continuing-education students are still served separately from curriculum students, but even this wall is beginning to crumble. In any event, the needs of emerging students are forcing change in traditional instructional delivery, and this process frequently will require leadership change.

The Emerging Leadership Mandate

Identifying what leadership characteristics are needed to create or continue a student-focused environment depends on many factors. Of course, if it's working already, don't fix it. More often than not, however, every college's leadership core can use some refresher courses. A college's receptivity to change, a clear understanding of students' needs, and the leader's perceptions of how to lead for change are paramount. Each college will have to determine what makes its situation unique and design leadership strategies to meet emerging student needs.

When faced with major changes, some colleges reorganize; others revisit mission, vision, or values statements; others develop new master plans; and others, unfortunately, do nothing. Regardless of the method used to address needed changes, the process is more valuable than the product. Getting the campus community together to focus on a common goal or problem and take ownership of it will ultimately be more important than a reorganization, mission shift, or master plan. Heightened communication, personal involvement, and understanding the issues will motivate faculty and staff members to change. People modify behaviors when they understand the need for modification and see its benefits. But they also must feel comfortable with making changes. The process of building relationships results in greater trust, which supports greater risk taking. When people feel comfortable taking risks to try new methods for serving students, they will blossom into more creative and innovative employees. Of course, the leadership tone is set for the entire college by the governing board and the president. The board should adopt a clear vision, the president must communicate it clearly and consistently, and its ownership should be shared by all.

The authors' leadership survey indicated the emergence of some innovative practices. Jerry Moskus reported that Lane Community College has implemented a collegewide restructuring process to provide better customer service by dissolving the bureaucratic pyramid of organizational "branches" into four groups of dynamic assemblages of similar teams. According to Moskus, "Categories that now divide the college community, i.e., credit vs. noncredit and transfer vs. non-transfer courses, are deemphasized in favor of greater collaboration and flexibility." He suggests that this organizational change is already having positive results. "The walls are coming down. People are changing their behavior. Lane is becoming more collaborative, more service oriented, less bureaucratic."

Dr. Jerry Sue Thornton, president of Cuyahoga Community College, Ohio, reported that her college adopted a continuous quality learning project with the support of its trustees. This activity involves up to twelve collegewide teams that review institutional processes, including three which deal directly with student outcomes. Thornton attributes team building, trust, and collaboration as those leadership attributes which encourage people to expand their roles and stretch beyond their current performance.

Internal leadership in a college only begins with the president. Leadership is the responsibility of every employee regardless of job function. This model should have two undergirding bywords: excellence and students. All employees should insist upon excellence in their job performance and focus completely on their primary customers: students. Presidents and other administrators should learn to value their subordinates and trust them to make more decisions that directly affect students. Faculty will have to move from teacher-centered instruction to student-centered instruction, and staff members will have to learn to make more decisions on their own and provide focused support to the teaching-learning process. In short, if the process of serving students becomes an obstacle, employees throughout the college should be empowered to deviate from or change the process. An open, trusting environment built on solid relationships and mutual professional respect will provide the appropriate climate for continuous change to meet the ever-shifting needs of students and communities. This should be the common goal of all community colleges.

STAYING COMMUNITY-CENTERED

To be community-centered, each college employee should understand the college's relationship and responsibility to the community. Each person who works at a college serves at the pleasure of the governing board, which in turn serves at the pleasure of and is responsible to the community. Colleges exist to contribute to the health of their communities' residents through educational development. They were created to be community-based organizations that seek out and respond to education and training needs. Colleges exist of, by, and for the communities they serve. Communities do not exist to serve colleges.

As they fulfill their missions of helping people develop educationally, colleges contribute to the greater good of the whole community. Carver's admonition to make sure that the "good produced by the college exceeds the cost of the college" should haunt all leaders daily (1994). They will focus on the community as a whole only if they understand their responsibility to it. Although they are stewards of the taxpayers, it is more important for them to see themselves as stewards of the community's health and the well-being of its people. Their responsibilities are to train a world-class workforce, educate tomorrow's leaders, help the disenfranchised, and make their communities better places in which to live. Community colleges provide important services designed for the greater good.

The question on everyone's mind is, "How can they be all these things to all these constituent groups?" This is not a new question. It has been an issue since communities began seeking direct help from community colleges with emerging social and business issues. The answer for most has been collaboration.

Collaborative Leadership

Collaborating with other community agencies and business became the model for most colleges in the eighties. Partnering with business to maintain state-of-the-art equipment, with public agencies to leverage scarce resources and donors to build endowments, likely will become even more important as colleges move into the new century. These collaborations don't happen automatically. All employees should constantly build good will for the college and watch for possible partnerships. The resulting synergy often broadens the financial base of the college, provides better information resources, and builds greater community support. These relationships become especially important during construction bond referendums and mill-levy increase requests.

External leadership initiatives are particularly important in building good community support. External leadership is built on trust and solid relationships, just as is internal leadership. Each employee and student should be a good ambassador for the college, but community leadership rests with the governing board, the president, and key community liaison staff, such as the corporate and continuing education dean. Governing board members, foundation trustees, and the president should be making friends, networking, and partnering whenever and wherever they can. A good strategic marketing plan is important, and public events, artistic performances, and community meetings on campus yield great dividends. However, there is no substitute for having good friends in key leadership positions throughout the community and state. Elected officials, power brokers, respected community leaders, and citizens at large should be nurtured continuously. Pueblo Community College, Colorado, recently benefited from a four million dollar estate left by an obscure but most benevolent property owner. He was simply befriended by the college and invited to become involved in its activities.

Internal relationships must also be developed continuously. As colleges mature, they evolve into a comprehensive collection of values, premises, relationships, and work ethics. This climate demands constant attention and support. Communicating from division to division, department to department, and among individuals is every bit as important to the college's health as is communicating with external entities.

The Rotarian call for "building good will and better relationships" could not be more applicable than it is to community colleges. Without the trust, support, and respect of fellow workers, community colleges cannot serve students and the community. The most heralded leaders will not lead effectively if their campuses have unrest, distrust, and contentiousness. A focus on employees' needs and interests is in this respect just as important as focusing on those the college is commissioned to serve. There are no secret recipes or perfect models to achieve and maintain campus harmony. Each employee, beginning with the president, must constantly work toward achieving a college's vision through open, honest, and fair communication.

Building relationships becomes a burden for any president who expects to do it all alone. It is doubtful that any one person can. Empowering others and using board and foundation members to help with external relationships are essential. In the end, internal and external leadership should be shared. By leveraging all the human resources at hand, the college's students and the whole community will benefit.

Dr. Norm Nielsen, president of Kirkwood Community College, Iowa, described a similar restructuring for better efficiency. "We have encouraged the use of multidiscipline staff task teams to tackle problems and opportunities facing the college. Our most recent college organizational chart has done away with the normal box diagram and characterizes our organizational structure in a cyclical, interactive fashion."

Dr. Phil Summers, president of Vincennes University, Indiana (a two-year community college), recently led his school through a comprehensive vision-development process in which each area of the institution developed a statement that supports the college's mission and vision. The preamble to their centerpiece publication "Power for the Future" is especially appropriate for all leaders facing the new century's challenges:

> Vincennes University celebrates its 200th anniversary in 2001. Our founding principles are the bedrock upon which we will build our future.
>
> We believe in the worth of the individual, the importance of education, and the value of service.
>
> Demographics change. Societal needs evolve. Accountability from our funding sources increases. Flexibility and creativity are imperative. We recognize the dynamic world in which we operate and will aggressively meet the challenge to be the innovative leader in access, opportunity, and success as Vincennes University enters its third century of service.

Several respondents to the survey emphasized the realization that community colleges must see themselves not merely as educational institutions, but more importantly as service businesses—with missions, customers, and competitors. Santa Fe's Dr. Lawrence Tyree stated, "Amid all the trendy acronyms, I believe our mission boils down to one thing: Are we serving our customers well?"

Dr. Chuck Carlsen, president of Johnson County Community College, Kansas, reported that his college uses a number of cross-functional terms to encourage innovation and that the college has adapted customer-service programs for training all front-line employees.

America's community colleges favor structures and operating procedures that focus on student and learner outcomes. Eliminating bureaucratic structures in preference of cross-functional teams and a common vision focused on students presents an exciting challenge for community college leaders of the new century.

CHAPTER 10

Team-Building Leadership

"Truly successful teams are managed and led. Although management skills enable teams to advance successfully through each stage of development, leadership skills inspire individual team members to realize their full potential at each stage" (Bennis and Nanus, 1985).

Community college leaders face new challenges in this time of rapid change in technology, information, the labor force, and the economy. Future managers will have to exercise leadership in an increasingly turbulent environment. These rapid shifts are difficult to see, analyze, and understand. Researchers explain that human cognition limits what one person can sense and comprehend. However, they state that each person is different, not only in viewpoint, values, and thinking mode, but also in limitations. What one person lacks another may possess, and what that person misses yet another may have. If only the minds of several people could be combined.

It is the wish for compounded vision and talents—several talented minds rolled into one—that drives writers and researchers to project that, in a turbulent future, the ideal leader will not be a solo superhero who makes all the right decisions and tells others how to carry them out. It will be someone who knows how to find and bring together diverse minds that reflect variety in their viewpoints, thinking processes, and problem-solving strategies.

THE TEAM-BUILDING LEADER

This view of leadership is not new. However, despite a long tradition of shared collegial leadership, few leaders have the necessary skills. Team-based leadership is apt to be more cognizant, alert, understanding, competent, talented, acceptable, efficient, equitable, and supportive than leadership by one person (Eisenstat and Cohen, 1990). In a complex work setting, group effort increases efficiency and effectiveness. Team building is essential to supporting and improving the effectiveness of small groups and task forces and must be a key part of community colleges' future. It also improves the effectiveness of work groups by focusing on setting goals and priorities, deciding on means and methods, examining the way the group works, and exploring the quality of working relationships.

A cycle develops of data collection and sharing, diagnosis, planning, action implementation, and behavioral evaluation. Interestingly, these skills are also required in Dr. Edward Deming's now famous plan-do-study-act (PDSA) cycle, regarded as the foundation of the quality movement practiced in many businesses and some educational institutions.

PROFILE OF A WORK TEAM

Not all work groups are teams. A.J. Reilly and J.E. Jones (1974) list four essential elements of teams. First, the members must have mutual goals or a reason to work together. The members of an effective department must share goals and an overall purpose. Second, there must be an interdependent working relationship. Individual faculty members are responsible for specific expertise and assignments, but must depend on other members. Third, individuals must commit to the group effort to maximize overall effectiveness. Finally, the group must be accountable to a higher level within the organization. The team will usually operate within the framework of a higher organization such as a division.

The team's overall objective is to control organizational change. This involves increased decision-making and problem-solving efforts. A primary objective of team building is to increase awareness of the group process. Group members will learn how to control change externally by experimenting internally. The effort will concentrate on barriers to effective functioning and develop strategies to overcome them.

Team-based structures or decentralized initiatives that fail often result from poor "followership," not leadership. There are few opportunities to learn how to be an effective member of a democratic group. A team member is one of a group of mutual followers. Members of effective teams will:

- Understand and commit to group goals
- Be friendly, concerned, and interested in others
- Openly acknowledge and confront conflict
- Listen to others with understanding
- Include others in decision making
- Recognize and respect individual differences
- Contribute ideas and solutions
- Value others' ideas and contributions
- Recognize and reward team efforts
- Encourage and appreciate comments about team performance (Pfeiffer, 1991)

The sequential pattern—alternating task and relationship behaviors—is the starting point for developing a model of team building.

THE TEAM-BUILDING MODEL

Tuckman's (1965, pp. 384-392) five-stage model of group development is "forming, storming, norming, performing, and adjourning." Other theorists enhance the team-building model to be sequential, thematic, and developmental. The model has five stages that occur in order, each with a general theme that describes group activity, and each stage must be accomplished and its problems resolved before movement to the next. The model includes task- and relationship-oriented behaviors and reflects the elements and characteristics of teams listed earlier.

Stage One: Awareness

The "forming" stage involves the task objective of orientation and the relationship objective of dependency resolution. Awareness is an overall theme. Team members need to understand and become committed to groups and to be friendly, concerned, and interested in others. They must begin by getting acquainted with one another. Unique identities and skills are important resources to be shared to create feelings of acceptance.

However, getting acquainted is not enough. There are many groups in which members feel comfortable with one another and know strengths and weaknesses, yet accomplish nothing. Therefore, the initial task activity is setting goals. This gives meaning to the team's existence. Members need to understand how the team fits within the organization, and how they are related to the team's goals.

The desired outcomes for the first stage are commitment and acceptance. These are critical to team development and prerequisite to the next stage.

Stage Two: Conflict

The "storming" stage of group development involves confronting resistance and the relationship objective of resolving feelings of hostility. Conflict emerges naturally. Team-building behaviors at this stage include acknowledging and confronting conflict openly at the task level and listening with understanding to others at the relationship level. Desired outcomes in this stage are clarification and belonging.

It is important at this stage that individuals listen attentively and actively, suspending assumptions, to all viewpoints. The diversity of shared opinions provides the team with a vital source of group energy. Team members develop an atmosphere that encourages and supports the expression of opinions and fosters a sense of belonging.

By encouraging expression of all disagreement and dealing with it, a team further clarifies its purpose and begins to define its most effective means for working together.

Stage Three: Cooperation

The "norming" stage involves the task objective of promoting open communication and the relationship objective of increasing cohesion. The overall theme is cooperation. Appropriate behaviors are to include others in decision making and to recognize and respect individual differences. The desired outcomes in the third stage are involvement and support.

As collaboration becomes a team norm, a feeling of genuine support develops. Members become more able to give and receive feedback, gaining a better perception of where they stand and more involvement in decisions.

Stage Four: Productivity

The "performing" stage involves the task objective of solving problems and the relationship objective of promoting interdependence. The general theme is productivity. Team members are encouraged to contribute ideas and solutions and to value the contributions and ideas of others. Desired outcomes for this stage are achievement and pride.

In team building, members work collaboratively to achieve objectives and are challenged to work to their greatest potential. A major concern at this stage is sustaining momentum and enthusiasm. Complex goals and objectives require the creation of incremental milestones. These establish success points and allow for celebration when they are reached. They contribute to motivation and team revitalization.

Stage Five: Separation

The "adjourning" stage may occur when a task is completed or when new team members are added. Some ongoing groups do not conclude at the fifth stage but recycle to stage one without adjourning.

The task objective is recognizing and rewarding team efforts, and the relationship objective stresses encouraging and appreciating team performance. The desired outcomes of the final stage of team building are recognition and satisfaction.

An evaluation of team accomplishments provides important feedback regarding task performance and working relationships. This documentation can be used to plan future ventures involving other teams. It also provides closure for the group and allows individuals to say good-bye or commit to further collaboration. This stage is a final celebration that includes recognition and satisfaction.

Although team development is presented as a process in which members are mutual followers, the context in which team building occurs requires the facilitator or team leader to thoroughly understand the leadership process. Administrators who persist in conventional practices of focusing on the thinking and agenda of just one person are likely to grow less effective as the world changes around them. One strength of a team lies in the members' ability to think together in ways that most individuals cannot. Thinking together means learning together by reflecting on individual practices, team experiences, and the experiences of others outside the team who must live within the realities defined.

TRANSACTIONAL AND TRANSFORMATIONAL LEADERSHIP

W. Bennis and B. Nanus (1985) suggest that the difference between transacting and transforming is the difference between managing and leading. Leaders, they say, influence and inspire others through value-driven vision; persuasive, anecdotal communication; and the development of a strong, predictable self. Managers lead by employing the skills necessary to get the job done. Truly successful teams are managed and led. Although management skills enable teams to advance successfully through each stage of team development, leadership skills inspire individual team members to realize their full potential at each stage.

Both forms of directing are critical if task and relationship outcomes are desired. Team members require more transactional leadership during the early stage of group life (and low levels of follower readiness) in order to achieve the team-building outcomes of commitment, acceptance, clarification, and belonging. Increased transformational leadership is required as the team develops and matures. The team-building outcomes of involvement and support require equal amounts of transactional and transformational leadership. Finally, in the advanced stages of group development and readiness, more transformational leadership is required to bring about the team-building outcomes of achievement, pride, recognition, and satisfaction.

To bring about the desired outcomes of the team-development process, the team leader needs to master specific skills and teach them at the right time to team members. Although all of these skills are needed and used all the time, a special group of skills is needed at each stage of team development.

While this type of leadership is appealing, it is extraordinarily difficult to achieve, and requires sustained dialogue among persons whose views may be in conflict. Four leadership capabilities essential to team building are understanding the subjective experience of others, sharing and interacting, criticizing, and reflecting or learning through reflection (Bensimon and Neumann, 1993). The attainment of real teamwork requires leadership's best efforts. Teamwork requires attention to processes often taken for granted. It also requires a deep commitment to follow through on processes that are hard to grasp and hard to talk about. Real teamwork also requires that people unlearn their old definitions of leadership and view it as a collective, interactive process.

CHAPTER 11

Planning for Change

*"The test of leadership is whether the fol-
lower and the organization are enhanced or
diminished by the leader's actions" (Sergiovanni, 1990, p. 53).*

CHANGING THE PARADIGM

The need for a completely integrated planning process is based in the new world in which society lives. The former view of the world and organizations, based on Newtonian physics, was as simple machines. That view has been replaced by quantum physics and chaos theory, which see these as complex systems.

As a simple machine, a college can have its dysfunctional units replaced without affecting other mutually isolated parts. As an open, complex system, a college must have its units and functions balanced simultaneously in a dynamic model forming a three-dimensional image.

The Newtonian view lends itself to quick fixes and linear planning. However, most challenges organizations face are complex and have no simple, unique solutions, nor can any one leader be expected to have all the expertise and information to solve them (Ackoff, 1993).

DEFINING STRATEGIC PLANNING

The difference between what passes for planning in American institutions and the Japanese method is that the Japanese start out saying, "Where should we be in ten years?" American planners focus most of their attention on the short-term. WCC differentiated strategic planning from annual planning by stating that strategic plans cannot be accomplished in a single year; rather, they are plans that change direction in response to WCC's external environment. Strategic planning is also different from long-range planning because it does not create incremental change. Strategic planning is designed to improve targeted areas and is not intended to change everything in an institution. In the strategic-planning process, an organization focuses on its mission and plans to realize its vision for the future. Pfeiffer and Jones say strategic planning helps an organization create its future.

The strategic-planning process should be regarded as organizational learning—through a participative planning process, the institution learns about itself and how it may improve. It is a powerful tool for helping individuals and organizations learn from the past and for projecting this forward in a future-oriented mindset. Community colleges need strategic planning because economic conditions, community expectations, competition for resources, and other factors change rapidly in today's world. Deciding which combination of choices to develop into a strategic plan is one of the most far-reaching and complex problems a college and its leadership will face.

It seems logical to begin planning with the mission and strategic directions. However, it makes little sense to plan the future direction of the college if the staff mistrust one another and refuse to share crucial information, expose their assumptions, or commit themselves to new directions. If the organizational culture is not supportive and trust has not been developed, the plan cannot succeed. The focus for the institution must be based on the core values and beliefs of the employees while redirecting organizational resources to meet community needs. Tom Watson, president of IBM, says of a long-lasting organization, "I think you will find that it owes its resiliency not to its form of organization or administrative skills, but to the power of what we call beliefs and the appeal these beliefs have for its people" (Reavis and Griffith, 1992, p. 111).

A vision approach takes two photographs of an institution: one for the future and one for the present. It is a dynamic picture of the future state of the college. It is more than a dream or set of hopes: it is a commitment. The vision provides context for developing strategic goals and recognizes the need to continue with the visioning process, even after the vision is produced.

It is important for leaders to define the types of relationships desired for the end state and, separately, those necessary to manage the period in which all change takes place. Choosing an appropriate change map helps top management. Diagnosis must be made not only of what the relationships are now but what form they will take in the changed state, with an integrated plan for change to bridge the difference.

Margaret Wheatley (1993) writes about vision as an "energy field." Vision coupled with commitment generates intensity that is magnetic!

Reavis and Griffith itemize the steps in planning for strategic change as need identification, strategic-response selection, information gathering, preparation, initiation, development, adoption, implementation, support, evaluation, and revision. They summarize this as a holistic approach, emphasizing that the total plan for change must be developed involving all aspects of the organization: budget, personnel, curriculum, instruction, decision making, culture, and so on (1992, p. 27).

There are three important questions to ask when beginning
a strategic planning process: At what stage do the needs of
students and the community require the college to be? How
will it get there? What will staff receive for helping out? It
is important to start out from the outside. The organization
that starts out from the inside and then tries to find places to
put its resources is going to fritter itself away. Above all,
it's going to focus on yesterday. One looks to the outside
for opportunity, for need (Drucker, 1990, p. 46).

Community colleges frequently begin a planning process from within. However, the needs of students drive effective strategic planning. Five themes pinpoint the focus of fundamental change efforts for institutions: mission or social purpose, identity or public perception, degree of satisfaction of key stakeholders, change in the way of achieving work, and change in the culture (Beckhard and Pritchard, 1992).

A strategic plan is a list of decisions that fundamentally changes the direction of an institution. It is much more precise than a broad statement of vision or mission. Its specific approaches are chosen to achieve a greater degree of effectiveness in serving the community, financing services, targeting a population, and changing the internal climate. For example, should the college develop a magnet-school approach? Should regional centers be virtual or real? Should technology be upgraded so staff have more efficient ways of operating? Should more effort be put into reaching at-risk students?

Formal planning documents constitute the psychological contract between each individual and the organization concerning what behavior is expected and what behavior will be rewarded (Kilmann, 1989). While this plan is subject to negotiation and change, it is important to document it so it can be understood and discussed.

Drucker lists common planning mistakes:

- Going from plan to full-scale operation. Don't omit the Deming idea of testing or piloting.
- Relying on what everybody already knows. It is probably out of date.
- Following a rigid strategy.
- Patching up the old rather than going all-out for the new.
- Repeating how it has always been done instead of examining what the issue requires.
- Assuming there is one correct strategy.
- Trying failed methods over and over. After a second try, move on to something else (1990. p. 71).

Drucker relates an old saying that "good intentions don't move mountains, bulldozers do. The mission and the plan—if that is all there is—are the good intentions. Strategies are the bulldozers." Strategies or action plans are not something to hope for; they are something to work for, he asserts. "Leadership is accountable for results.... It isn't just thinking great thoughts, it isn't just charisma; it isn't play-acting. It is doing. The first imperative of doing is to revise the mission, to refocus it, and to build and organize, and then abandon. It is asking ourselves whether, knowing what we now know, we would go into this again" (1990, p. 59).

Planners must see interconnected contributions to realizing the vision, instead of a series of improvement projects laid atop one another. It is important to understand the relationship between the culture of the future, structure of the organization, allocation of work, information systems, and employees' sense of meaning in working there. The strategic interface considers how well the plan has been derived for all stakeholders, then translates into organizational objectives and tasks. If the strategic interface is not properly aligned, subsequent effort is devoted to designing the wrong tasks. Efficiency has no meaning if effectiveness is not achieved.

The structural interface considers how well the troublesome task flows have been placed within rather than among subunits. The job interface considers how well subunit managers guide their subordinates to spend the right amount of time on the right tasks.

Kilmann writes that college leadership will choose to realign strategy and structure for the future only if the college has developed an adaptive culture and built in a learning approach to the strategic planning process; if top management's efforts include a review process as a regular part of its own working style; and if all its members learned the skills for managing dynamic complexity.

After the strategic document is prepared, managers must "tell and sell" the plan until all members of the institution understand how they fit within the new directions and how the plan will change their work. Written and verbal communication must be regular, frequent, and face to face. Making the strategic plan operational means members who are assigned tasks must be given the financial technical, material, and informational resources to turn plans into action. If the organization's strategic potential is to be achieved, every member must be provided with an operational structure to guide his or her time and effort, including objectives to be pursued, tasks to be performed, and management that coordinates all work units into a functional whole.

William Glasser's latest book, *The Control Theory Manager* (1994), combines Deming's quality concepts with his control theory, resulting in the following advice to those he labels as "lead managers": Lead managers have followers and do not need to push their employees. According to Glasser, they engage the employees in honest discussion of the cost and the quality of the work; show and model the job so that employees can see exactly what the manager expects; eliminate most inspection; and continually teach the employees that the essence of quality is constant improvement.

The first unit chosen for change should be a mission-directed unit. If the purpose is to spread planned change throughout the organization, then the chosen unit should be critical to the college's success. The plan develops and specifies the way in which change will spread throughout the organization.

Ralph D. Stacey (1992) writes that control through planning behavior proceeds in clearly laid-out steps: discovery (formal analytical scanning of the environment), choosing an objective setting and plan formation, plan implementation, and a return through formal monitoring to discovery.

Here, behavior is constrained by organization, intention, relation to objectives, and planned routes to them. The pattern of action produced is regular movement toward the objectives.

According to Stacey, planning and monitoring activity is a system of control. Control by planning is a structural approach with the advantage of clarity but the disadvantage of inflexibility. Control by ideology is a flexible behavioral approach but is less measurable from the center. The aim is to secure regularity in the pattern of behavior and help the organization adapt to its environment. In both cases, control is implemented through feedback loops. Both assume a reasonably close link between causes and effects, and between actions and their outcomes. In a dynamic environment, long-term control has to take a different form. Only through creating a climate in which complex learning occurs and healthy political interaction thrives can open-ended change be planned.

> Value added leadership emphasizes leadership rather than
> management; enhances meaning rather than manipulates
> situations; enables subordinates rather than gives directions; builds an accountability system rather than installs a
> monitoring system; develops collegiality rather than congeniality; and leads with passion rather than calculation.
> Leadership is an offer to control. The follower accepts this
> offer with the understanding that this control will not be
> exploited. The test of leadership is whether the follower
> and the organization are enhanced or diminished by the
> leader's actions (Sergiovanni, 1990, p. 53).

CHAPTER 12

The New Century Board of Trustees

"A vision is a dream created in our working hours of how we would like the organization to be" (Peter Block, 1987, p. 102).

A college's success requires visionary leadership at all levels, but especially among governing board members. Their role in policy development and in driving the mission, vision, and goals of their colleges is critical to continued strong, customer-based services. America's community colleges are at a crossroads in their development. Intervention and strong direction by governing boards to restore the achievement-based, customer-driven nature of their colleges are essential to a competitive and economically healthy society.

Community college governing boards must reassess or reaffirm their missions relative to the divergent and growing demands of the economy and determine the most appropriate methods for meeting them. These boards and their CEOs should also present a clear vision of what these colleges aspire to become.

This transformation process should be driven by them, and the responsibility for leading these institutions ultimately rests with them. With the changes in society, the economy, and the perception of higher education, governing boards must be prepared to lead effectively to prevent a catastrophe. A board can begin its mission for 2000 at various spots in the road; however, the path of political strategy is an important first step.

POLITICAL POSITIONING STRATEGIES

College trustees have an obligation to lead their respective institutions into the most favorable political climate possible. Most educators are unlearned in political positioning, and public educators are sometimes restricted from direct political lobbying by statute or school policy. Trustees, and their president or chancellor, represent a powerful potential for affecting their institution's future in the political arena. The following political activities are often successful:

Develop allies before you need them. Trustees and the CEO should continuously identify people who are able to affect their institutions and develop social relationships with them. Visits from those trustees most able to influence the targeted politicians, business leaders, or power brokers are always most successful. These relationships, of course, should become long-lasting and genuine.

Get involved in public policy development. It is much better to be involved in the development of state or federal policies than to simply react to them. Trustees and college officials should endeavor to be appointed to boards and commissions that most affect the college's ability to fulfill its mission. Every state, for instance, has a job-training coordination council.

Become ambassadors for the college. Trustees, above all else, should be thought of as the primary ambassadors for the institutions they represent. Those with the best business connections should be strong advocates for the college's workforce development efforts. Widespread exposure and familiarity with business leaders, economic development officials, and job-training directors are most important. When a new college president arrives, these are the people he or she should meet first.

Use trustee-focused organizations. A number of these are excellent resources for the political positioning process. The Association of Governing Boards and the Association of Community College Trustees are two excellent national groups. Many states have equally active associations. Regional accreditation agencies and program-specific agencies also represent good information sources. The publications of all these organizations—such as AACC's recent Trustee Guide for Carrying the Community College Message to Congress—are most instructive regarding the political process. Among scores of specific lobbying activities, the essential elements of effective political positioning include providing a quality service based upon the needs of your constituents and solid friend-raising.

A Time for Reassessment

It is prudent to recognize that the missions of community and technical colleges vary for many good reasons. It is equally prudent that missions should be reviewed often, particularly at publicly supported schools, to assess whether they are in concert with the needs and interests of taxpayers. Many social institutions and organizations have gone the way of the dinosaur or saber-toothed tiger because of an arrogant refusal to change. The visionary community college will survey the needs of its constituents and adjust accordingly. The visionary governing board will demand such periodic reassessments.

Unfortunately the broad-focused mission of community colleges creates an image problem. The general public often appears confused about the purpose of two-year colleges and their significance to society. With few exceptions colleges are still not recognized for their positive local economic effect. The basis for this confusion is their multifaceted missions. Two-year colleges are expected to fill the gap between secondary education and the university by including services in college transfer, technical/professional training, continuing education, corporate education, adult-literacy education, ESL, and adult basic education. Astute boards and administrators still deliver such services, but have selected the technical-professional and business elements for greatest public emphasis. As a result these colleges gain local and statewide prominence and leverage additional resources to help fulfill the remaining elements of their missions. It is this business integration activity that the general public, business community, and elected officials understand and appreciate.

Fortunately, most community colleges have learned to be market-driven, needs-based, and client-centered because their missions prepared them for close partnerships with business. Their technical/vocational programs have been driven by business' needs since their inception, largely through the use of business advisory committees. Unfortunately, community colleges were structured after the university model, and as they matured, they began to resemble universities by becoming more insulated, bureaucratic, and self-centered rather than customer-centered. Many colleges must reconcile their missions, particularly in better balancing all of their services. Other colleges simply need to develop a clearly focused vision statement which complements a broad mission statement. CPCC recently held a board of trustees retreat to develop such a vision statement. Its mission statement is:

> Central Piedmont Community College is an innovative and
> comprehensive public two-year college with a mission to:
>
> > • advance the lifelong educational development
> > of adults consistent with their needs, interests,
> > abilities, and efforts; and
> > • strengthen the economic, social, and cultural
> > life in the Charlotte-Mecklenburg region of
> > North Carolina.

Its vision statement is:

> CPCC intends to become the national leader in workforce
> development.

The college is attempting to become more customer-driven and has adopted two litmus-test questions to be asked before any new policy, procedure, or program is implemented. These questions are: Is it good for our students? Is it good for our community?

A Time for Accountability

As successful as some of them have been in workforce development, community colleges dare not coast. The preponderance of America's manufacturer-based workers are classified at the "technical" level—that is, those requiring more than a high school degree, but less than baccalaureate-level skills training. This represents a tremendous market, but to grab it many colleges need to move to a higher and more responsive level of service to business. This will require an institutional commitment to offering programs at business workplaces and in their employees' homes. It will require self-paced, technologically based instruction that focuses on the student, not the teacher. And it will require lasting partnerships with business interests. Management training, skills training, employee screening and assessment, and employee retention training represent some of the most fundamental services community colleges should provide to local workers. There may always be a need for and an interest in teacher-centered, lockstep education, but seldom is this kind of delivery effective in business sectors. The time for visionary leadership in America's community colleges has never been more needed.

It is no longer acceptable to simply design training programs, recruit students, and teach classes. Today's community colleges must be equally concerned with retraining students through the successful completion of their programs of study and with placing them in meaningful employment. It is not enough for teachers and administrators to be responsible for the teaching-learning process. They must be equally concerned with whether students secure or maintain employment in their selected fields and are successful in their jobs. This nation depends on community colleges as its primary workforce training source. They can no longer afford to provide a service without post-product accountability.

A Time for Building Better Relationships

Colleges cannot be expected to meet the emerging workforce challenges alone. The nation's K–12 school districts have a fundamental role, and examples of delivery systems and curricula are being piloted all over the country. America is still a "nation at risk," but there is evidence of genuine concern and serious attempts to reduce that risk. As elementary and secondary schools reassess their goals for student achievement and how students can best attain them, the question of postsecondary choice quickly emerges. Until recently, there were only two choices for high school students and their counselors to consider: college "prep" or general education. Prep students were selected almost exclusively based on grade point averages and received more rigorous training in mathematics, science, and the humanities. All other students were funneled into the ill-defined general-education program, which produced questionable results. College prep students presumably would become white-collar workers, and general education students presumably would become blue-collar workers. In a 1960s-model economy, these presumptions and artificial stratifications might have been acceptable, but in today's global marketplace they are barriers to producing employees with the critical thinking and technical skills necessary for economic competitiveness.

To meet his new challenge, Parnell spearheaded the concept of "tech prep." This concept of two years of high school technical preparation followed by two years of community or technical college preparation is spreading across the nation with enthusiasm. With a curriculum based on knowledge and skills needed by employers, the tech prep programs provide the basics for lifelong careers and connect education directly to the workplace. The system gives high school students a viable alternative to general education or even basic training in a trade.

Community colleges and their boards must work closely with K–12 districts to drive the college prep and tech prep curricula, and to articulate course transfer and course development with high schools in a meaningful and responsible fashion. Through this type of interaction and support, America will begin to benefit from a cohesive, market-driven, needs-based educational system that will keep it productive, competitive, and economically strong.

POLICY ISSUES—MISSION AND VISION

Whenever great social change is needed or perceived to be needed, there is an overwhelming tendency to expect change overnight. When change is slow and irregular, as with American education reform, societal frustration leads to demands for change by government legislation. However logical this may seem to government policymakers and their supporters, it is inherently bad for everyone. National mandates generally do not allow flexibility for local or regional needs, and the resulting programs inevitably become so entrenched and bureaucratized that any future adjustment to meet emerging needs is impossible.

To prevent this, governing boards must adjust their missions to meet current and future needs. Their renewed missions must then drive the preferred curricula and educational delivery systems. Often the mission statement is still relevant, but a fresh vision statement will help to refocus and reenergize the college as a needs-based, customer-driven institution. A true vision statement will set the course for what the organization desires to become. It establishes high expectations and represents the collective consciousness of the college. A shared vision becomes the will, indeed, the powerful resolve of the college. This is strong evidence that a shared vision may be the single most important attribute of any successful organization. Jim Collins, a Stanford Graduate School of Business faculty member, extols the success of visionary organizations. His research indicates that visionary companies, going back to 1926, performed fifty-five times better than the general market (Brown, 1992).

Peter Block (1987, p. 107) describes a vision as a "dream created in our working hours of how we would like the organization to be." A mission statement, according to Block, is simply a statement of what business the organization is in. He cautions that even if leaders create a vision, it is up to each employee, in the context of the organization's mission, to create his or her own vision of the future.

This monitoring and evaluation is the board's most important job. Federal, state, and local statutes must be reviewed and lead to changes as necessary, and regional accreditation standards, where applicable, should be factored into the process. The most important component, however, is to scan the external environment, including local constituencies and employers, to determine current and projected needs. This entire process should take into account the legal, social, economic, and political dimensions associated with change.

Next, the internal or campus environment should be surveyed to determine the acceptability of the proposed changes and seek input for developing a new vision. Internal barriers to change should be identified and plans developed for overcoming them. The college community, especially faculty, must participate in developing a shared vision which they understand and can embrace. Finally, strategic plans for implementing the changes must be developed to include a thorough awareness of the associated internal and external social, political, economic, and educational implications. Such changes are not easy, especially in higher education, but are essential to maintaining organizational success and helping this nation keep pace with its economic competitors.

The following activities are recommended to any college that seeks change in its mission or vision statements:

1. With governing board approval, conduct a review of the literature regarding statement development and reassessment.
2. Solicit external and internal opinions on the college's mission and the needs of its students and of the community.
3. Conduct a retreat with the governing board and the executive leadership team to focus on one strategic issue—mission (or vision) reassessment. A professional facilitator is often effective, but not essential. Presentations by state, regional, and local planners are most useful. Develop a proposed statement that addresses the major values or needs represented by the surveys suggested in step two.
4. Review the proposed statement with all those involved with the college, including the college attorney, elected officials, business people, students, faculty, community leaders, area educational systems and agencies, accrediting bodies, and the editorial boards of significant news media.

5. Adopt the new statement (which hopefully includes direct references to corporate education, economic development, and/or workforce development).
6. Publicize it internally and externally.
7. Secure for the college president the financial and political backing to implement the change and require that all master plans, institutional goals, value statements, and effectiveness plans support the new statement.
8. Provide staff development activities necessary to maintain faculty and staff support.
9. Evaluate and publicize the resulting activities and outcomes.

Policy development, especially the establishment of mission and vision, becomes the primary instrument for organizational growth and change. If a college hopes to remain focused on the needs of customers, students, employees, and the community at large, it must embrace the concepts of quality service and the continuous improvement of service.

A Time for Change

The popular comparison of the life cycle to organizational development is particularly relevant to community colleges because most of them have now matured to the point of decline. In their "birth" years (the 1960s), there was much excitement, experimentation, and enthusiasm. In their "growth" years (the 1970s), innovation and expanding enrollments created a synergy that brought respectability and fulfillment. In their "maturing" years (the 1980s), a focus on quality and partnerships produced continued growth and a higher level of comfort. Many of today's community colleges have already entered the "declining" years (the 1990s), which produce self-centered, isolated environments in which organizations grow less effective at serving their customers.

This typical organizational development process generally results in further deterioration unless a renewal process intervenes. Today's mature colleges not only face the decline expected in the development cycle, their customers' needs also have changed dramatically. Communities' social demands have accelerated, and businesses' education and training needs have increased like never before. These two compelling forces make it essential for governing boards and CEOs to intervene with the renewal or reinvention of achievement-based, customer-driven organizations.

A renewed mission or vision statement sets the theme and drives the behaviors of college people. These fundamental statements (or expectations) eventually affect all areas, including organizational structure, marketing activities, programs, and services. Any such effort that lacks the governing board's full support and involvement undoubtedly will fail.

Trustees must not only accept their role as ambassadors to the community, they must act as ambassadors for the community to the college. Their responsibility is to determine what the community most needs and to develop the college's goals accordingly. They must act in the best interests of the community and the college, with an emphasis on the community and its residents. It is important for the college president to provide appropriate training opportunities for board members so they clearly understand their important responsibility as primary stewards of the college and its services to their community. The bottom line is that the governing board and the president must be socially accountable as the institution's primary leadership team.

CHAPTER 13

Instructional Design and Content in the New Century

> *"The successful community colleges in the twenty-first century will be colleges where faculty members can demonstrate that their teaching strategies are in fact 'causing learning'" (George A. Baker, 1994, pp. 205-217).*

This is a critical time in this country's history—a time when America's people and her businesses need educational services more than ever. Fortunately, the body of literature on this call for greater accountability and responsiveness is growing. The fundamental processes of teaching, curriculum development, and instructional delivery must be looked at in new ways. As the people's colleges and the premier developers of the workforce, community colleges must be worthy of the challenge. They must be willing to restore the teaching and learning activity as their unmistakable priority. In doing so, its leaders must also be willing to change the curricula and the delivery of instruction to be more accountable to their customers.

Adjusting processes and services to meet current and anticipated customer demands is an imprecise and challenging activity. America's businesses became well acquainted with "reinvention" during the past decade as they tried to compete better in their markets. America's community colleges are facing the same challenges and are at a pivotal point in their development. Will they evolve into insulated organizations like many of the universities after which they were structured, or will they evolve into dynamic community-based, customer-driven colleges that wish to meet the needs of the new century?

There is a fundamental truth about organizational behavior community colleges should recognize; that is, any public organization that doesn't remain accountable for its services will soon be held accountable by its customers or its governing body or both. Worse yet, a competing organization will seize unserved, potential customers through better, more accountable services, and the affected organization will lose its specific market category forever.

TEACHING AND LEARNING: THE CORE MISSION

A Nation at Risk (National Commission on Excellence in Education, 1983) set off a remarkable series of local, state, and national initiatives to improve America's education systems. After many false starts and some notable successes, the federal government has adopted some meaningful National Education Goals, published in *America 2000: An Education Strategy* (U.S. Department of Education, 1991). Not surprisingly, the common denominator throughout these goals is the teaching and learning process.

It is sad that this national interest in education reform had to come from outside education—specifically, the government and business. Community colleges have always emphasized teaching and learning as their fundamental mandate and, in particular, have prided themselves on their accessibility and accountability. Yet in most instances, these champions of teaching and learning have not excelled in measuring the effectiveness of their teaching or in providing flexible schedules and curricula as needed by their students and those who employ those students. Community college leaders may have been diverted from this primary mission in their zeal to build campuses and secure resources to operate them. In his latest book, Terry O'Banion (1994, p. 5) states, "Leaders now have a clear mandate to place teaching and learning at the top of the educational agenda in order to repair the neglect of the past and prepare for a new future beginning in the year 2000." Community colleges dare not think themselves immune from this national demand for better student outcomes and increased instructional accountability.

Albert Lorenzo and Nancy LeCroy (1994, pp. 6, 10) write that the time for fundamental change is when society's needs can no longer be met by the institutions which serve it. They accurately suggest that "the overall goal for the community college is to create a culture of responsiveness that more clearly relates its comprehensive mission to these new societal circumstances." And there it is: a succinct, clear statement of what community colleges should be about. Developing a strategy to respond to the needs of today and of the new century will present some interesting and exciting challenges for community colleges throughout the nineties.

A Framework for Teaching and Learning

There is no perfect structure or framework for propelling a community college effectively into the twenty-first century. Guiding a college into the future is much like steering an ocean liner across the Atlantic. The captain has to continuously monitor the seas, the weather, and navigational data to correct the ship's course. Even the best-laid plans, for ships or community colleges, simply chart an intended course based upon the best data available. Situations and circumstances change, and the course of ships and community colleges should change with them. The secret is to ensure that the plan is strategic and flexible within the parameters of the institution's mission and vision.

If a college intends to meet changing needs, its people must be willing to change. Trustees can effect policy changes and administrators can effect process changes, but any significant shifts must occur where customers are served—with instructors. Faculty must be willing to shift paradigms and embrace change as a constant. This is not a new concept, but it has surfaced regularly in the eighties and nineties. William Deegan and Dale Tillery (1987, pp. 36-40) write, "The challenges to the community college mission, the developments in technology, the needs for developmental education, the problems of a largely 'tenured in' and immobile faculty and staff, and the changing needs of American society will all be powerful forces for institutional and individual adaptation." Contributors to George Baker's recent publication (1994, pp. 603-614) repeatedly stress the need for institutional and individual change, faculty included. For example, Albert Smith concluded his contribution by stating:

> The focus in community college teaching, as well as in all of higher education, needs to move away from teacher behavior to student behavior/learning. The successful community colleges in the twenty-first century will be colleges where faculty members can demonstrate that their teaching strategies are in fact "causing learning."

Daniel Phelan summarized his chapter by calling for greater responsiveness to meet constituent needs by faculty, staff, and administrators. Teachers must begin to respond more to students and their communities, and administration and staff must be willing to support them in this.

Most of today's community college instructors recognize that change is inevitable. They are forced to do more with less; increase peripheral duties like advising, recruiting, and committee work; and become computer proficient. Many seek change, while others avoid it altogether. Nevertheless, all faculty will have to develop a new mindset and versatility of skills if they hope to remain effective in the new century. The old concept that faculty should be "managers of learning" as opposed to "dispensers of knowledge" has really come of age. The instructor for the future must become a Renaissance teacher. Job duties of the future instructor will include at least the following descriptors: information specialist, performer, job placement specialist, advisor, media producer, media performer, mentor, computer whiz, mediator, budget specialist, TQM expert, collaborator, recruiter, networker, and learner.

Instructors will face perhaps the most exciting times of their careers if they accept the challenge to evolve into professionals with vision and adaptability. They have the opportunity, if not the imperative, to be relieved of routing schedules, campus-based teaching, and business as usual. They will have unprecedented access to information via electronic networks and on-call data bases, allowing contextual learning to flourish. They will get to expand their student bases by teaching at workplaces and satellite locations throughout their service areas. Some will even be able to teach from their homes or from hundreds of miles away via distance-learning technology. Tomorrow's faculty will be in perpetual renewal. This portends an exciting, dynamic profession in anybody's book.

However, none of this renewed enthusiasm, this rejuvenation, will be realized unless faculty who have become self-focused resolve to become more community- and student-focused. The issues of the day must shift from workload and academic freedom to flexible schedules and learner outcomes. The support systems for teaching must also be transformed, and trust between administrators and faculty must increase.

COLLEGES OF THE TWENTY-FIRST CENTURY

Much has been written about successful leadership and management among America's businesses, in particular that organizational structures and management philosophies are not working as well as they did during the developmental years. If leaders expect faculty to become completely customer-oriented and flexible, they must empower teachers to become what society demands. The best way to do this is for administrators and support staff to set the example. Someone will ultimately be responsible for college activities, but the case for empowering people, especially faculty, has been well established. The problem is that not many people, administrators or faculty, really know how to be effective at it yet. However, no one knew how to be effective at serving adult learners in the sixties or existing workers in the seventies, yet community colleges eventually became the nation's experts. Hopefully they also will become better at pushing decision making to the lowest levels and working effectively with leadership teams.

The time is ripe for all colleges to reassess their missions, visions, and goals. A thorough master-planning process can be an effective means for institutional renewal or even reinvention. Whatever mechanism is used, colleges must provide support systems for effective teaching. Continuous scanning of student, employer, and community needs is equally important if faculty are expected to succeed. Administrators and support staff must view their roles as service agents for the faculty. Administrators should remove obstacles from instructional processes so faculty can better serve students. Staff development and performance assessments should be intricately linked and driven by instructor and learner needs. Everyone must value the students, whether they take credit or noncredit curricula. Everyone must see their mission as part of a larger whole, as part of a greater good. Above all is the need for trust and professional respect among all employees. The community created the community college, and the community is what the college should most wish to serve.

CURRICULUM DEVELOPMENT

The common observation that "the more we change, the more we seem to be the same" is true of colleges in most respects. It is not an indictment, but a validation that colleges have always felt the need to be responsive, even proactive, at meeting the needs of their students and communities. Jim Gollattscheck (1994) cites a 1922 declaration of the membership of the American Association of Junior Colleges that reads: "The Junior College may, and is likely to, develop a different type of curriculum, suited to the larger and ever-changing civic, social, and vocational needs of the entire community in which the college is located."

Community colleges now find themselves in the information age. This is quite a leap from the industrial age spoken of in 1922 by the founders of today's AACC. But today's emerging demands are no more challenging to us than those of the twenties were to them. Curricular needs are diverse and resources are limited. The real difference for two-year colleges of the nineties rests with the way they see themselves. No longer can students be expected to meet college schedules and take prescribed curricula. No longer can they be expected to flourish in a teacher-centered environment. The successful community college sees itself as customer-focused and part of a greater community. Lorenzo and LeCroy capture this notion by observing that moving toward a holistic perspective is a prerequisite to creating a culture of responsiveness.

However, colleges must not abandon the basic principles and values of the curricula. The basics of the work ethic, responsibility, and respect for others should remain imbedded, whether courses are credit or noncredit, or taught on campus, in the workplace, or telecast to homes. Reform to meet emerging needs will involve process and content adjustment, but the ethics of teaching and the integrity of the curricula should remain.

New Curriculum Content and Processes

Delivery of instruction is already undergoing tremendous change. However, the process for developing most new curricula is a dinosaur from decades past. The faculty are the "keepers of the curriculum," but cannot expect it to be relevant when they develop it in a vacuum. With the possible exception of the general education core, the college's customers should have major input to curriculum development. Employers should drive the skills development courses, and community and business leaders should have some input regarding the general education core. Academic standards must, of course, remain high. Finally, all new curricula should be developed in modular format with identified outcome measures, displaying maximum flexibility for delivery and measured student achievement.

Modularized, measurable curricula will pave the way for diverse delivery and exciting entrepreneurial development. America's business leaders could care less about college semesters or lockstep schedules. Most business executives—and their workers—have no interest in the credit versus noncredit issue. They just want what they need when they need it, at their place if possible, and have little patience with educational traditions, policies, or fiscal regulations. They rightly see themselves as taxpaying customers.

In most parts of the country, corporate training is the community college's fastest-growing market. Corporations and small businesses have become a major customer base, and colleges should develop curricula that are flexible enough to serve it. Students also are becoming more sophisticated in their demands, and we see more faces of, say, working mothers in their thirties, who endure the serious challenges of adulthood and are growing impatient with archaic rules and regulations. Again, the requisite is for flexible curricula. Colleges must influence legislated changes, if necessary, to provide the flexible services demanded by their customers.

As community colleges adapt, curricular change will drive new behaviors. The concepts of semesters and quarters will vanish, as will the division between credit and noncredit services. Consider the choices of an ice cream lover. He or she can have it in any variety of flavors, in a cup, a cone, or a box, or can get it in stores and vending machines all over town. Why shouldn't students be able to learn mathematics customized to their needs from a variety of sources: on campus, at work, or at home? Ice cream is ice cream, whether it is served in a cone or a cup, chocolate or vanilla. Mathematics is mathematics, whether it is taught on campus or at work, whether it is algebra or statistical process control. Corporate and continuing education "shadow colleges" should be integrated with the credit components of community colleges. As colleges concentrate on becoming externally focused, the old barriers and division walls will tumble.

For faculty, workloads could suddenly involve a diversity of professional-growth options like never before. A math instructor might teach two credit courses on a central campus, a statistical process control course at a corporate site, and develop an interactive video disc on Ohm's Law with a colleague from the electronics department. Sherrie Kantor, dean of corporate and continuing education at CPCC, compares this concept to the development of "math stores" or "science stores," where college customers can pick and choose from a directory of skills. As technologies merge on college campuses, so too must the credit and noncredit curricula merge, requiring fundamental change in thinking and funding. For instance, a credit course should not be considered more valuable and funded at a higher level than a noncredit course of equivalent length, subject, and teacher credentials. Such merging will require an emphasis on trust-building and relationship-building among faculty, staff, and administrators.

Finally, any future curriculum development must factor in the interests of society. International education is becoming a cultural norm for most urban colleges. Extensive English preparatory programs have sprung up almost overnight. Literacy education, diversity education, and critical-thinking skills must be considered as societal interests evolve. For example, rebuilding neighborhoods and teaching parenting skills are now emerging as new mandates for community colleges. Colleges must broaden their horizons with respect to serving their customers. This is an exciting time. It is a time for enthusiasm.

INSTRUCTIONAL DELIVERY

America is facing a number of critical issues from multiple fronts. In their zeal to provide services to anyone who needs them, community colleges have achieved a blurred image and a reputation for trying to be all things to all people. This zeal has produced an entrepreneurial and collaborative approach to education, but in the process community colleges have been perceived as the alternative colleges or colleges of second choice. Part of this perception is driven by an American culture which values that which is exclusive, like universities. How can community colleges gain widespread community and legislative respect and support when they are open-door institutions?

Successful business leaders know just how to deal with such a dilemma. They scan the marketplace, choose to produce or provide the products and services where they can be the best, and focus entirely upon serving their niches. It is not unrealistic to transfer this business approach to community colleges. To maintain the status quo or chart a rigid course for the future is tantamount to institutional suicide. The concept of adopting a more flexible approach for serving niche customers may be oversimplified, but it allows for greater concentration on what community colleges do best: teaching. Colleges can shift gears and alter their course as customer needs and societal interests change. They can and should expand their comprehensive mission, but they must maintain and protect teaching excellence. Teaching will simply be packaged and delivered in many different ways, based upon the needs of their customers.

Although many will continue looking to community colleges to fill the gap between public schools and universities with every conceivable social program, colleges can emphasize those component services which they determine will best serve their students and the whole community. The ability to deliver these services in a timely, convenient, and effective fashion will become most important as student and community demands increase. Community colleges now face a workforce training imperative that requires much more than a course in self-esteem or TQM. It means literacy education, ISO 9000 training, academics, and everything in between. Companies recognize that people make their business, and understand that productivity is directly related to their workers' education and skill levels. Lifelong learning has become a universal cultural mandate. Student who prepare for first-time jobs are equally interested in timely, convenient, and quality education. They are less able to meet the structured requirements of on-campus, lockstep classes.

Community colleges boast about being needs-based and community-centered, but in reality they have become attracted to the notion that they are academic islands, worthy of admiration and respect just because they exist, modeling university behavior. Well, the gong has sounded, the trumpets are blaring. The call is for a more responsive educational system, and that responsibility rests squarely with community colleges. A shift to a true customer-focused organizational model will force them to improve at leading and marketing college services and to succeed for the long-term good of students and communities. It is unlikely that K–12 will be able to change much; their plates are so full of social demands, change will be slow no matter how much clamoring is done in state legislatures. And most universities have no interest in meaningful change. Therefore, it is up to the community colleges. This opportunity should begin and has begun in many places, with more accountable instructional delivery. By modularizing curricula, colleges can offer menus of instructional offerings to diverse customers. These options might include lockstep campus courses and collaborative courses; lockstep off-campus courses; service learning courses or labs; scheduled or pay-per-view telecourses; interactive video discs or videotapes; interactive distance learning; radio broadcasts; ITFS or wireless cable courses; customized corporate courses; information highway courses; and human interest courses. The list could expand ad infinitum, but the point is valid. America's community colleges must rethink how they are doing business and serving their customers if they hope to continue contributing meaningfully to their constituents, including the taxpayers who support them.

Fortunately there are signs of cultural change, which normally begins with leaders, at community colleges across the country. The authors' leadership survey reveals some exciting examples of leadership growth. David Ponitz, president of Sinclair Community College, Ohio, reported that besides reading current leadership theory and practice, he regularly attends WorkBank presentations on interactive cultures and leadership. Other presidents, like LCC's Jerry Moskus, regularly attend professional leadership training workshops presented by Glaser and Associates, Stephen Covey, and Zenger-Miller. Norman Nielsen, president of Kirkwood Community College, Iowa, has been trained in Total Quality Control and is implementing its principles in his college. Vincennes' Phillip Summers has already implemented a shared leadership practice by leading the school through the development of a comprehensive vision document.

There is reason for optimism and good cheer. Community college leaders are aware of the need to become more oriented to the needs of customers and the community at large. Creating new visions and restructuring processes and organizations to achieve those visions are what leadership in the new century is all about.

As people's needs change, America's community colleges also must be prepared to change. No single CEO or board of trustees can effect such institutional responsiveness alone. Those who prepare the curricula and deliver the instruction must embrace the attitude of being needs-based and market-driven. The most principled, transformational president, dean, or department chair in the country cannot adjust to meet emerging customer needs unless the faculty clearly recognize and agree to the vision of responsiveness. The notion of pushing decision making to the lowest levels in an organization is especially helpful to community colleges. Innovation and leadership should be encouraged at all levels. By working together in a climate of trust, community college professionals can and will recapture the commitment to customer service and recreate the legacy of those pioneering community-based colleges from which they came.

BIBLIOGRAPHY
Leadership in the New Century

Ackoff, Russell. "Mechanistic to Social System Thinking." Massachusetts Institute of Technology, 1993. Videotape.

Adizes, Ichak. *Corporate Life Cycles*. New Jersey: Prentice Hall 1988.

Baker, George A., ed. *A Handbook on the Community College in America: Its History, Mission, and Management*. Westport, Connecticut: Greenwood Press, 1994. pp. 205-217, 603-614.

Beckhard, Richard and Pritchard, Wendy. *Changing the Essence*. San Francisco: Jossey-Bass, 1992.

Beckman, Brenda M. and Doucette, Don. "Community College Work Force Training Programs: Expanding the Mission to Meet Critical Needs." Innovation Abstracts. League for Innovation in the Community College, Volume 6, Number 2. February, 1993.

Bennis, W. and Nanus, B. *Leaders: The Strategies for Taking Charge*. New York: Harper & Row, 1985.

Bensimon, Estela Mara and Neumann, Anna. *Redesigning Collegiate Leadership*. Baltimore: John Hopkins University Press, 1993.

Block, Peter. *The Empowered Manager*. San Francisco: Jossey-Bass, 1987, pp. 102, 107.

Brown, Tom. On the Edge with Jim Collins. *Industry Week*. October 5, 1992, p. 14.

Carnevale, Anthony P. "America and the New Economy." U.S. Department of Labor, Employment Training and Development Division. The American Society for Training and Development, 1991, pp. i-2.

Carver, John. "Reinventing Governance." Keynote address to the 1993 Association for Community College Trustees Convention. Toronto, Canada. Videotape.

Covey, Stephen R., Merrill, Roger A. and Merrill, Rebecca R. *First Things First*. New York: Simon & Schuster, 1994, p. 281.

Covey, Stephen R. *Principle-Centered Leadership*. New York: Simon & Schuster, 1991, pp. 18-19.

Covey, Stephen R. *Principle-Centered Leadership.* New York: Simon & Schuster (fireside edition), 1992, pp. 69, 250-260.

The Chronicle of Higher Education. December,1994.

Deegan, William L. and Tillery, Dale. "Toward a Fifth Generation of Community Colleges." *Community, Technical, and Junior College Journal.* April/May 1987, pp. 36-40.

DePree, Max. *Leadership as an Art.* New York: Bantam/Doubleday/Dell, 1989, pp. 15, 16.

Drucker, Peter F. *Managing the Non-Profit Organization.* New York: Harper Business, 1990.

Edgerton, Russell. "The Engaged Campus: Organizing to Serve Society's Needs." 1955 National Conference on Higher Education Call for Proposals, American Association for Higher Education. Fall 1994, pp. 1, 2.

Eisenstat, R.A. and Cohen, S.G. "Summary: Top Management Group." In J. Richard Hackman (Ed.), *Groups That Work (and Those That Don't): Creating Condition for Effective Teamwork.* San Francisco: Jossey-Bass, 1990.

Eskow, Seymour. Speaking at the 1974 Rockland Community College Conference, New York, 1974.

Fisher, James L. "Reflections on Transformation Leadership." *Educational Recor.d.* Summer 1994, pp. 54, 60-65.

Gerstner, Louis V., Jr. *Reinventing Education: Entrepreneurship in America's Public Schools.* New York: Dutton/Penguin, 1994, pp. 1, 2.

Glasser, William. *The Control Theory Manager.* New York: Harper Collins, 1994.

Gollatscheck, James F. "The Community Focus of America's Community and Junior Colleges." Combase Monograph, 1994, p. 2.

Gonzales, Thomas. "American's Choice: High Skills or Low Wages." Leadership Abstracts, League for Innovation in the community College, Volume 3, Number 17, November 1991.

Green, Madeleine F. "Not for Wimps or Cowards: Leadership in the Post-Heroic Age." *Educational Record.* Summer 1994, pp. 55-60.

Greenleaf, Robert K. *The Leadership Crisis—A Message to College and University Faculty.* Newton Center, MA: The Robert K. Greenleaf Center, 1978, pp. 8-9.

Hammer, Michael and Champy, James. *Reengineering the Corporation.* New York: Harper Collins, 1993, pp. 5, 32.

Jacobson, Robert L. "Prodding Academia to Do More for Poor Children." *The Chronicle of Higher Education.* June 24, 1992, p. A5.

Kayser, Thomas A. *Mining Group Gold*. El Segundo, California: Serif, 1990, p. ix.

Kilmann, Ralph H. *Managing Beyond the Quick Fix*. San Francisco: Jossey-Bass, 1989.

Kolberg, William H. and Smith, Foster C. *Rebuilding America's Work Force*. Homewood, Illinois: National Alliance of Business and Business One Irwin, 1992, pp. v-vii.

Kotter, J. *Organizational Dynamics: Diagnosis and Intervention*. Reading, Mass.: Addison-Wesley, 1978.

Kouzes. James M. and Posner, Barry Z. *Credibility*. San Francisco: Jossey-Bass, 1993, p. 22.

Lofy, Chuck. *A Grain of Wheat*. Burnsville, Minnesota: Prince of Peace, 1993, p. 15.

Lorenzo, Albert L. and LeCroy, Nancy Armes. *A Framework for Fundamental Change in the Community College: Creating a Culture of Responsiveness*. Macomb Michigan, Macomb Community College Press, 1994, pp. 6, 10.

Maynard, Roberta. "A Web of Federal Timing Programs." *Nation's Business,* March 1993, p. 25.

Morgan, G. *Images of Organization*. Newbury Park, CA: Sage, 1986.

National Commission on Excellence in Education. *A Nation at Risk*. Washington, D.C.: National Commission on Excellence in Education, 1983.

O'Banion, Terry and Associates. *Teaching and Learning in the Community College*. American Association of Community Colleges, 1994. p. 5.

Parnell, Dale. *Dateline 2000*. Washington, D.C.: American Association of Community and Junior Colleges, 1990, pp. 103, 240, 250.

Pfeiffer, J.W. ed, "A Model of Team Building." In J. W. Pfeiffer, *Theories and Models in Applied Behavioral Science*. Vol. 3: Management/Leadership Series. San Diego: Pfeiffer & Company, 225- 257, 1991.

Pfeiffer, J. W. ed. *Theories and Model in Applied Behavioral Science*. Vol. 4: Organizational. San Diego, Pfeiffer & Company, 1991.

Polak, Fred L. *The Image of the Future*. New York: Oceana Publications, 1961, p. 43.

Reavis, Charles and Griffith, Harry. *Restructuring Schools*. Lancaster, Pennsylvania: Technomic Publishing, 1992.

Reicher and Schneider. "Climate and Culture: An Evolution of Constructs." In B. Schneider (Ed.), *Organizational Climate and Culture*. San Francisco: Jossey-Bass, 1990.

Reilly, A.J. and Jones, J.E. "Team-Building." In J.W. Pfeiffer & J.E. Jones (Eds), *The 1974 Annual Human Resources.* San Diego: University Associates, 1974.

Rummler, Geary A. and Brache, Alan P. *Improving Performance: How to Manage the White Space on the Organization Chart.* San Francisco: Jossey-Bass, 1990, p. 5.

Schein, Edgar H. *Organizational Culture and Leadership.* San Francisco: Jossey-Bass, 1992, p. 48.

Senge, Peter. "Applying Principles of the Learning Organization." Washtenaw Community College, Michigan. December 5, 1994a. Videoconference.

Senge, Peter. "Creating Quality Communities." *Executive Leadership.* Provo, Utah: Executive Leadership Publishing, June 1994b, Vol. 11, No. 6. p. 11.

Senge, Peter. *The Fifth Discipline.* New York: Bantam/Doubleday/Dell, 1990.

Senge, Peter, et al. *The Fifth Discipline Fieldbook.* New York: Bantam/Doubleday/Dell, 1994c, pp. 299, 300, 593.

Sergiovanni, T. *Value-Added Leadership.* New York: Harcourt Brace Jovanovich, 1990, p. 53.

Stacey, Ralph D. *Managing the Unknowable.* San Francisco: Jossey-Bass, 1992.

Szabo, Joan C. "Training Workers For Tomorrow." *Nation's Business* March 1993, pp. 22-32.

Tuckman, B.W. "Developmental Sequence in Small Groups." *Psychological Bulletin.* 63, 1965, pp. 384-392.

U.S. Department of Education. *America 2000: An Education Strategy.* Washington D.C., Department of Education, 1991.

Weick, K.E. "The Significance of Corporate Culture." In P. Frost, L.F. Moore, M.R. Louis, C.C. Lundberg and J. Martin (Eds.), *Organizational Culture.* Newbury Park, CA: Sage, 1990.

Wheatley, Margaret J. *Leadership and the New Science: Learning about Organization from an Orderly Universe.* San Francisco: Berrett-Koehler, 1993, p. 78.

Zuboff, S. *In the Age of the Smart Machine.* New York: Basic Books, Inc. 1988, p. 32.